CONTEMPORARY ITALIAN

FAVORITE

RECIPES

—— FROM ——

KULETO'S

ITALIAN

RESTAURANT

CONTEMPORARY ITALIAN

FAVORITE RECIPES
— FROM —
KULETO'S
ITALIAN
RESTAURANT

by Robert Helstrom

Photography by John Vaughan

An Astolat Book
HARLOW & RATNER
Emeryville, California

Library of Congress Cataloging-in-Publication Data
Helstrom, Robert, 1957–
    Contemporary Italian : favorite recipes from Kuleto's Restaurant /
by Robert Helstrom ; photography by John Vaughan.
      p. cm.
    "An Astolat book."
    Includes index.
    ISBN 0–9627345–7–8 : $24.95
    1. Cookery, Italian. 2. Kuleto's Restaurant (San Francisco,
Calif.) I. Title.
TX723.H46 1993
641.5945 – dc20   93–1690
                                           CIP

Printed in Singapore
10 9 8 7 6 5 4 3 2 1

Harlow & Ratner
5749 Landregan Street
Emeryville, CA 94608

Photographic Styling: Jody Thompson-Kennedy
Book and Jacket Design: Daniel McClain
Illustrations: Susan Mattmann
Typography: Classic Typography and Ted Hayashi's Typography

Props for Photography:
Aletha Soule, Sebastopol, CA, pg. 47, 51, 62, 76, 84
Biordi, San Francisco, pg. 67, 68, 80, 89, 107, 128, 133, 134
Cyclamen, Berkeley, CA, pg. 43, 64, 101, 140
El Plato, San Francisco, pg. 83, 89, 108, 114
Fillamento, San Francisco, front and back cover, pg. 45, 50, 88, 120, 131, 144, 165
Hastings & Hastings, Mill Valley, CA, pg. 29, 67, 101, 107, 114, 118, 128, 133, 148, 156
Jimtown Store, Healdsburg, CA, p. 19, 38
Manderley, San Rafael, CA, pg. 108, 160, 162
Carlo Marchiori, Calistoga, CA, pg. 30, 37, 76, 97, 101, 128
Pullman & Co., Mill Valley, CA, pg. 47
Sue Fisher King, San Francisco, front and back cover, pg. 45, 48, 50, 54, 62, 73, 76,
83, 84, 88, 92, 116, 120, 128, 131, 137, 139, 144, 151, 152, 155
The Gardener, Berkeley, CA, pg, 45, 92, 110, 144
Wilkeshome at Wilkes Bashford, San Francisco, pg. 59
Williams-Sonoma, San Francisco, pg. 80

Special thanks to: Far Niente Winery, Maria Miranda Gresham, Carlo Marchiori,
Denise Mondot, Robert Puccini, Sara Schmitz, Pete Sittnick, Sherry Viner

ACKNOWLEDGMENTS

Just as running a restaurant involves a lot of individual efforts, many people have helped make this book possible. The entire staff of Kuleto's restaurant is really responsible for helping create something worth writing about. However, a few individuals need to be singled out.

The dessert and bread recipes are the work of Pastry Chef Denise Mondot. Denise has been at Kuleto's longer than I have, in fact from the very beginning, and her commitment and contribution to the overall success of the restaurant goes beyond the delicious breads and desserts that come out of the pastry station.

Thanks also to our sous chefs through the years, particularly David Machado and Debbie Allen. Dave was my right hand for several years before moving on to Pazzo in Portland, Oregon, and then Debbie took over without missing a beat. I always knew I could leave the restaurant in their hands with complete confidence that things would be done just the same way as if I were there.

I especially want to thank the whole kitchen staff, the ones who are there in the trenches day in and day out making the whole thing work. Their dedication and commitment to quality is the real backbone of the restaurant.

Pete Sittnick came aboard as General Manager at just about the same time I did, and it has been a pleasure working with him as both the front and the back of the house have continued to grow and evolve.

Thanks also to Bob Puccini, vice president of Kimco Hotel and Restaurant Management Company, for giving me the perfect blend of artistic license, encouragement, and constructive criticism to keep the restaurant always on the right track.

As my editor, Jay Harlow made this project easy for me. He brought his experience both as a cook and as a writer to help me translate restaurant techniques to home recipes, and to get my thoughts down on paper. I hope I taught him some new things; I know I learned things from him. Publisher Elaine Ratner was always there to remind both of us of what the average cook does and doesn't know.

I am grateful to photographer John Vaughan for his artistic eye and his excellent photos. It's a pleasure to see this food in such varied and beautiful settings. Thanks also to Jody Thompson-Kennedy, who showed up each day with an enormous amount of props, flowers, and fabrics to make sure we had just the right ones for each dish. And to Susan Mattmann for her clear, instructive, elegant drawings.

Jerry Wilson gave me my first kitchen job about twenty years ago. Over the next five years, he taught me the restaurant business from the bottom up, and gave me the discipline that has made my career possible.

Finally, I want to thank my wife Denise for her constant support throughout my career. I know it's not easy being a chef's wife.

To Mom,
who taught me to love to cook,
and Dad,
who said "Whatever you choose to do,
do it well."

CONTENTS

INTRODUCTION
CONTEMPORARY AMERICAN-
ITALIAN COOKING

Why "American-Italian"? Because "Italian-American" implies a person of Italian ethnic origin living in America, which I am not. Reverse the term and to me it means something else, namely the kind of restaurant we have and the kind of cooking we do—inspired by centuries of tradition in Italy, but at home in the U.S. in the late 20th century.

Judging by restaurant openings, articles in food magazines and newspapers, and the selection of foods available in grocery stores, Italian cooking is more popular than ever in the United States. Partly that has to do with long-term changes in the way we eat and think about food. One of the healthiest trends in American cooking in decades is the growing influence of the "Mediterranean diet"—a way of eating based on grains, vegetables, and fruits, olive oil and wine, and a modest consumption of meat.

Not only is most Mediterranean food good for us, it's also full of exuberant flavors. Sun-ripened tomatoes, eggplant, and peppers, fragrant herbs such as basil and thyme, citrus fruits, and garlic are just a few of the flavors that show up repeatedly throughout the cuisines of the Mediterranean countries. Of all of these, including Spanish, Provençal, Greek, Turkish, Middle Eastern, and North African, the most popular by far with Americans is Italian.

From its beginnings in 1986, Kuleto's has been part of a new generation of Italian restaurants in America. Until recently there were two main kinds of Italian restaurants in this country, "southern" (although they rarely referred to themselves that way) and "northern" (which proudly proclaimed themselves as such). The first formed the postwar American image of the typical Italian restaurant: red check tablecloths, Chianti flasks for candle holders, posters of Venetian gondolas next to posters of Sicily, garlic bread loaded with grated cheese, and lots of tomato sauce. The "northern" restaurants, on the other hand, were designed like temples of gastronomy, with plenty of white linen and gold trim, waiters in tuxedos, and tons of butter and cream. In fact, many older restaurants with Italian names seemed to look away from Italy, combining French and sometimes Viennese dishes with Italian under the heading of "Continental cuisine."

Somewhere along the line, a growing number of Americans (including many chefs) became aware that Italian cuisine is a much more complicated subject. They began to take a closer look at the many regional cooking traditions of Italy, as well as the *nuova cucina* that has transformed contemporary restaurant cooking in Italy much as the *nouvelle cuisine* movement did in France.

What we at Kuleto's are doing represents a middle ground between the old poles of north and south. Most of our dishes represent northern styles, but we often look south for ideas. (If our style draws especially on any particular region of Italy it is probably Tuscany, with its simple grilled meats, excellent olive oil, and vegetable and bean dishes. The southern boundary of Tuscany, Umbria, and the Marches also marks the usual division between southern and northern Italy.) We rely heavily on olive oil, but we're not afraid to use butter and cream when the food tastes better that way. We use southern-style dried pasta (macaroni) for some dishes, northern-style fresh egg noodles for others, according to which works better in a given dish.

All the time, we are filtering these traditions through modern American sensibilities. We don't expect that all our customers will order a traditional Italian multi-course meal (antipasto, pasta, entree, salad). If a diner wants just a salad and a dish of pasta, that's fine. If you want to skip all the starters and go straight to an entree, fine. You can even make a whole meal of an assortment of antipasti.

We are fortunate in the variety of ingredients available to us. Now we can get authentic Italian radicchio and *prosciutto di Parma*, which were unavailable here just a few years ago, as well as a wider selection than ever of Italian wines, cheeses, olive oils, and other basics. We are also free to use many ingredients that are not traditional in Italian cooking, such as salmon and dried cherries, or to use traditional ingredients in non-traditional ways, as in making our basic vinaigrette with balsamic vinegar.

Whenever you depart from tradition, you risk stepping on some toes. One of the hazards of my job is occasionally being called out to the dining room to be grilled by a customer who is very knowledgeable about Italian food traditions. In Italy, I have been told on more than one occasion, linguine with clam sauce would never contain pancetta. Another customer may say a fresh tomato sauce like the one on page 81 goes only with thicker cuts of dried pasta, never angel hair. All I can do is nod in agreement, then explain that we do it the way we do because our customers like it.

Those of you who have eaten at Kuleto's should find recipes for your favorite dishes in the following pages, plus a sampling of our ever-changing repertoire of daily specials. And to those who have not yet been to the restaurant, we look forward to seeing you next time you are in San Francisco. In the meantime, I hope you will enjoy our contemporary American-Italian cuisine at home, and that you will serve these dishes to family and friends with as much pleasure and pride as we do at Kuleto's.

Robert Helstrom
San Francisco, 1993

11

THE AMERICAN-ITALIAN KITCHEN

—— INGREDIENTS AND BASIC RECIPES ——

MENU PLANNING, AMERICAN-ITALIAN STYLE

COOKING TECHNIQUES AND EQUIPMENT

INGREDIENTS AND BASIC RECIPES

MENU PLANNING,
AMERICAN-ITALIAN STYLE

One of the big differences between Italian and American-Italian styles is the pattern of meals and menus. The traditional Italian meal (usually the midday meal or *pranzo*) is a succession of courses, often beginning with an appetizer (*antipasto*). Next comes a first course (*primo piatto*) of pasta, risotto, or soup, which is followed by the entree or *secondo* of meat, poulty, or fish. Salad is served after the entree, and dessert is typically just fruit and cheese. You can certainly order that way in an Italian restaurant here, but because American restaurant portions are geared to a different pattern of eating, you are likely to get an awful lot of food.

If you look at the typical Italian meal, you see a balanced assortment of meat, vegetables, and grains, but you don't necessarily get them in the same course. Americans, on the other hand, tend to like everything on the plate together, Thanksgiving dinner style: meat, potatoes, vegetables, sometimes even salad. We try to balance the two, putting perhaps more on our entree plates than a diner would expect to find in Italy. (See the introduction to the entrees chapter on page 118 for more on how we compose our entree plates).

Because of these different backgrounds, many Americans eating in Italian restaurants (both here and in Italy) either don't know how to order a typical multi-course meal or, more importantly, choose not to. If there is a typical dinner pattern at Kuleto's, it would be an antipasto (often shared by two or more people), followed by a salad, and then either an entree or a pasta, and usually dessert. Others may order a pasta to split, then go on to their entrees. Lunches are typically just two courses, starting with antipasto or salad and following with pasta or an entree.

If we tend to order fewer courses in a restaurant than Italians do, the difference is even stronger in home cooking. I know that I rarely eat as many courses at home as I do when dining in a restaurant. If we are having pasta and a salad, they both hit the table at the same time, family style. It's only when we are entertaining that we are likely to plan the menu in courses, with at least an antipasto to precede the main course.

The quantities and number of servings in this book, then, are based on an American-Italian style of menu rather than the traditional Italian. Most of the pasta recipes, for example, serve two as a main dish, but are suitable as a first course for four. The entrees are generally larger than they would be in Italy, because we assume they will not always be preceded by both an antipasto and a *primo*. If you want to serve a succession of courses, the recipes given here will go farther.

FOLLOW THE SEASONS

For the best-tasting, most affordable meals, keep your menus in tune with the seasons. Some foods, like cultivated mushrooms and dried beans, are available all year, but most produce and many meats and seafood have definite seasons. Artichokes are never better or less expensive than in late winter, and that's when we feature them most prominently. Thanks to air freight and the demands of the most expensive hotel and restaurant kitchens, you can get fresh asparagus from somewhere or other any time of year, but my advice is to save the asparagus dishes for those couple of months in spring when it is at the height of its season. To really taste the flavor of tomatoes, peppers, and eggplant, wait until they arrive in local farmers' markets in late summer, then go ahead and enjoy them in every way possible.

Cooking Techniques and Equipment

Most if not all of the recipes in this book can be made with the tools found in any well-equipped home kitchen. You will need an assortment of pots and pans, including at least one good-sized (10-inch or larger) saute pan with a heavy bottom. Heavy aluminum is the best choice, with an anodized or stainless steel finish if you can afford it. A 10- to 12-quart pasta pot with a perforated insert that allows you to lift the finished pasta out of the cooking water is handy, and can double as a stock pot. Otherwise, you will need a large colander for draining cooked pasta. A food processor makes many tasks easier, from making pesto to mixing pasta dough, although I have specified some places where a blender actually works better.

A few recipes call for more specialized equipment. Making your own fresh pasta (see page 71) is easiest with a pasta machine, either hand-cranked or electric (but not the extruding type). A meat grinder is necessary if you want to make your own sausage, plus a stuffing attachment if you want to put the sausage in casings. The breads and some of the desserts are much easier to make with a heavy-duty tabletop mixer, but they can be made with hand tools and elbow grease.

SAUTEING

None of the cooking techniques is beyond the skill of the average home cook, either. Other than grilling (see below), sauteing—cooking food quickly in a shallow pan in a small amount of oil—is probably the most important technique in the restaurant kitchen. The main difference between the way restaurant cooks and home cooks saute is a matter of heat. A barely warm pan on a moderate burner will not give the same searing effect as a thoroughly heated pan over high heat. Restaurant ranges are much hotter than home ranges, and we generally turn them up full blast. To get the closest thing to restaurant results, try to saute over the highest heat you can manage. Of course, your margin for error is smaller with higher heat, so you have to pay attention.

Organization is the key to successful sauteing, as it is to just about any cooking method. This means having all your ingredients cut, measured, and otherwise ready (what French chefs call *mise-en-place*) before you start to heat the pan. You don't want to have to stop in the middle of sauteing thin slices of veal to chop the shallots or rummage around in a drawer for the measuring spoons.

GRILLING

Grilling over an open fire is the oldest of all cooking methods, and an essential part of the true flavor of Italian cooking. The hardwood grill, about 6 feet wide and fired with oak logs, is the centerpiece of the kitchen at Kuleto's. We use it not only to grill meat, fish, and poultry entrees, but also to roast peppers for peeling, grill mushroom caps for antipasto, and toast slices of bread or polenta to garnish entrees.

As a home cook you can make the same multiple use of the grill. As long as you have a fire going to grill some fish steaks or lamb chops, you might as well roast some peppers or onions for future use, or grill some eggplant or zucchini slices to go with your meal.

Living in central California, I use my home grill almost all year, but especially in the summer. When I'm entertaining in the summertime the routine goes something like this: Having stopped at the store on the way home and picked up some fresh mozzarella or Cambozola, I fire up the grill about an hour before the guests arrive, then pick and slice some tomatoes. When the fire is good and hot, I roast some peppers for peeling, then some sliced eggplant, and as people arrive, toast some crostini or warm up a slice of focaccia (and assign a few tasks like peeling peppers to the earliest arrivals). Then I add some more charcoal for the main course and we sit around and enjoy our antipasto while the fire burns down to the perfect cooking stage again.

The grilled dishes in this book can be prepared on anything from a hibachi to a big built-in barbecue. If you have a fireplace that draws well, you can also grill indoors in cold or wet weather. (Let a fire of hardwood logs burn down to glowing coals, then use a couple of stacks of bricks to support a grill a few inches above the fire.) I leave the choice of fuel—hardwood, charcoal, or gas, smoking chips or grapevine cuttings for flavor—up to you.

Because every grill and every fire are different, it's hard to give exact instructions for grilling recipes. But here are a few general bits of

advice. First, build a bigger fire than you think you need. Nothing is more frustrating than trying to cook on a fire that is not hot enough or on a grill surface that is too small. If possible, build a fire so there are hotter and cooler areas of the grill; this allows you to sear the food on the hot spot, then move it to a cooler area to finish cooking. Finally, be organized, and be ready to cook during the half hour or less that the typical fire is at the perfect temperature for cooking. This is no time to be cutting up ingredients or running to the kitchen for the salt shaker. If cooking several items at once, figure out which ones can hold for a few minutes at the edge of the grill and which need to be served immediately.

If grilling is impossible, most of the grilled dishes in this book can also be cooked under a broiler. You'll miss the slight touch of smoke and the special taste that comes from drippings sizzling on the hot coals, but the food will still have the attractive look and flavor that comes from high direct heat.

Ingredients
and Basic Recipes

Good cooking begins with good ingredients. Most of the ingredients in the recipes are familiar to Americans and are available in most cities. A few are harder to find, and may require a trip to a well-stocked delicatessen or other speciality food shop. On the following pages are notes on how to select, store, and use many of the ingredients called for in this book.

Also included here are recipes for some of the sauces, stocks, breads, and other basic preparations which show up throughout our menu and throughout the book.

AIOLI

Sauces made of pounded garlic and olive oil are found all along the Mediterranean coasts of Italy and France. In Liguria, the stretch of Italian coastline closest to France, the version called *agliata* is bound with bread crumbs. I prefer its Provençal cousin *aioli*, which is thickened (like mayonnaise) with egg yolks. It may be less authentic, but it goes so well with seafood, meats, and vegetables that it has become a standard part of our menu.

A basic recipe for aioli follows, along with some flavored variations. Like other egg-emulsion sauces, aioli can be made by several different techniques, using equipment from the simple (a bowl and whisk) to the sophisticated (a blender or a food processor). We begin with the low-tech version, which doesn't even require a mortar and pestle.

BASIC AIOLI

Makes 1 cup

> 2 large cloves garlic, minced
> 1 teaspoon kosher salt
> 2 large egg yolks (room temperature)
> Scant ¼ teaspoon white pepper
> 1½ teaspoons lemon juice
> 1 cup olive oil
> 1 tablespoon water, or more if needed

1. Place the garlic on a cutting board, sprinkle with ½ teaspoon of the salt, and mash with the side of a broad knife blade with a rocking, rotating motion until it forms a nearly liquid paste. Scrape up the paste with the knife and place it in a medium mixing bowl with the egg yolks, remaining salt, pepper, and lemon juice.

2. Beat the egg mixture with a wire whisk until pale and foamy. Add a tablespoon or so of the oil and beat until well incorporated. Repeat two or three times, whisking thoroughly each time, then slowly pour in the rest of the oil in a thin stream, whisking constantly. Toward the end, when the mixture becomes very thick, add a little of the water alternately with the oil. Taste for seasoning and adjust if necessary. For a paler color, beat in a little more water.

Variation: *Herb Aioli*
Stir 2 tablespoons chopped fresh herbs of your choice into 1 cup of Basic Aioli. Serve with vegetables such as the grilled potatoes on page 111.

Variation: *Caper Aioli*
Stir 2 tablespoons chopped capers, 1 tablespoon chopped tarragon, and 1 tablespoon minced shallots into 1 cup of Basic Aioli. Serve with Deep-Fried Squid (page 55) or other fried shellfish.

BASIL AIOLI

Adding a puree of fresh basil leaves results in a slightly thinner form of aioli, to be drizzled over foods rather than used for dipping. While Basic Aioli can be tricky to make in a blender, this one works fine.

Makes 1¼ cups

> Leaves from 1 large bunch basil
> (about 2 cups loosely packed)
> 1 cup olive oil
> 2 large cloves garlic, chopped
> 1 teaspoon kosher salt
> 2 egg yolks, at room temperature
> Scant ¼ teaspoon white pepper
> 1½ teaspoons lemon juice
> 1 tablespoon water

Wash the basil leaves and spin them dry in a salad spinner or pat them dry in a towel. Combine the leaves with ¼ cup of the oil and the remaining ingredients in a blender. Cover and blend at high speed until smooth. Add the remaining oil in a thin stream (through the feed hole if you blender has one) with the motor running. Taste for seasoning and correct if necessary. We serve this aioli with the Focaccia Crab Cakes on page 52. It's also good with grilled fish or cold shellfish, or drizzled into pasta dishes made with shellfish.

Variation: Sun-Dried Tomato Aioli
In place of the basil, use 8 reconstituted sun-dried tomato halves (about ¼ cup coarsely chopped), increase the water by a tablespoon, and reduce the total amount of oil to ¾ cup. Use with grilled meats or fish.

ARUGULA

Also known as rocket or roquette, this slightly bitter and hot-tasting herb is delicious both raw and cooked. It's closely related to mustard and horseradish; the big difference is that you can make a whole salad of arugula. We use it in salads along with other greens, or by itself as a garnish (it's especially good as an accompaniment to dry-cured meats like prosciutto and the Italian air-dried beef known as *bresaola*). Fresh arugula is fairly easy to find in bigger cities now, but it can be very expensive, especially when sold in small bundles with the herbs rather than among the salad greens. Fortunately, it's very easy to grow at home. Whether selecting it in the market or in the garden, choose leaves that are on the small side, and just beginning to show their lobed, oak-leaf shape; bigger, more deeply cut leaves are likely to be too strong.

BASIL

Basil is the first thing I plant in my summer garden, right along with the tomatoes. Whether you use just a bit of chopped or shredded leaves or make a whole handful into pesto, basil gives its unmistakable flavor and aroma to pasta dishes, salads, pizzas, and cheese-based mixtures such as the stuffing for Chicken Breast Stuffed with Herbed Ricotta (page 122). Except when it is necessary to add it to a dish early on, as in a stuffing, I prefer to add basil near the end of the cooking so it is still just releasing its perfume as the dish reaches the table.

There are many varieties of basil, including varieties with smaller and larger leaves, various colors, and flavor overtones of cinnamon, lemon, or anise. We use the familiar large green variety with smooth or lightly creased leaves, sometimes called "lettuce leaf" basil. There is no substitute for fresh basil; the dried herb does not have the same flavor or aroma. It's best when locally grown in the summer, but it's available all year from hothouses and warmer climates, and we use it throughout the year at the restaurant.

BUTTER

Butter in this book means unsalted butter, the type used in developing the recipes. It's the only kind we use in the restaurant. I find that even if I cut out the other salt called for in a dish, using salted butter can make the final result too salty.

CHEESES

The following varieties of cheese, some Italian and some from other countries, show up repeatedly in the recipes in this book. All of them should be available in specialty cheese shops, and you may find many of them in better supermarkets. Try to buy only what you can use in a week or two, and store them tightly wrapped in the door of the refrigerator.

Cambozola

A relatively new invention from Germany, this soft-ripened cheese with blue veins combines the qualities of Camembert and Gorgonzola (thus the name). It's delicious by itself, especially to those who find the flavor of Gorgonzola a bit strong. I like to serve a small amount of Cambozola with focaccia and roasted garlic as an appetizer. I also use it in a delicious sauce for grilled mushrooms and polenta (page 49).

Goat Cheese

A few of the recipes in this book call for fresh, unripened goat cheese. We use Laura Chenel's California Chèvre, partly because I like using locally made products, but also because I like this particular brand. There are other good producers of fresh goat cheese around the country, or you could use the French Montrachet.

Gorgonzola

A soft blue-veined cheese from Lombardy, named after a town near Milan. Like other blue cheeses, it's often served with fruit as a dessert course, but it is also traditional with polenta and in a few pasta sauces such as the tortellini recipe on page 74. The softer version (the type called for in the recipes in this book) may be labeled *dolcelatte* to distinguish it from the harder, drier aged version.

Mascarpone

Somewhere between cream cheese and clotted cream, mascarpone is simply fresh cream curdled slightly with tartaric or citric acid and drained of some of its moisture. The result is a smooth, sweet, very rich cream cheese with a slightly nutty flavor. We use the Galbani brand from Italy, and use it mostly in the dessert Tiramisú (page 149). It's also in a few savory preparations, including the smoked salmon ravioli on page 76.

Mozzarella

There is a huge difference between fresh mozzarella and the familiar packaged variety—so much that they are really two different cheeses in my view. The fresh version is higher in moisture and has a softer texture and lower melting point. Its butterfat content is also somewhat higher, since it is made from whole milk rather than part skim milk. And the flavor is much fresher and more delicate. Fortunately, fresh mozzarella is now more widely available than it used to be, from a growing number of high-quality domestic producers.

I always use fresh mozzarella in uncooked preparations and those in which the cheese is combined with hot ingredients only at the last minute. In summer, one of my favorite dishes is slices of fresh mozzarella with slices of ripe tomatoes and basil from my garden, drizzled with a bit of olive oil and sprinkled with salt and pepper. Formed into small balls (*bocconcini*) and served plain or marinated in olive oil with herbs, fresh mozzarella is a perfect addition to an antipasto platter.

Fresh mozzarella should be stored in liquid from the time it is made until it is ready to use. Look for stores that display it in its liquid and pack it that way for you to take home.

The one place I would use packaged mozzarella rather than fresh is on pizza; the fresh version releases too much water as it cooks, resulting in a soggy pizza.

Parmigiano Reggiano

This is the original "Parmesan," named after the city (Parma) and the province (Reggio Emilia) of its origin. You can easily tell it from other Italian grating cheeses (which go under the generic name of *grana*) because its name is stenciled all over the rind. Authentic Reggiano is the most expensive of the type, but I think it's worth it. The flavor is mild, rich, and mellow rather than harsh or excessively salty.

Parmesan is most familiar to Americans as a grated cheese, to be showered on pasta. But not every pasta dish needs it, and I have called for it only in recipes where it has something to add.

In buying cut pieces of Reggiano, look for a pale, creamy color and a texture which is still crumbly, not rock-hard. Keep it well wrapped in the refrigerator, and try to use it within a week or so.

A food processor is handy for grating Reggiano in quantity, especially when it will be melting into a dish rather than scattered on top. Just cut the cheese into smallish cubes, removing the hardest part of the rind, and chop it with the steel blade (not the grating disk) to the desired size. Stored in an airtight container, it will keep its fresh flavor for a couple of days. If the grated cheese won't be melted, for the best appearance grate it on a flat grater, preferably one which grates it into fine shreds. In some cases I prefer thin curls cut with a vegetable peeler to grated cheese.

Ricotta

This soft, fresh cheese looks like cottage cheese with an extra fine curd, but there is a major difference—it stays smooth when heated rather than turning into hard clumps. It's mainly used in stuffings and pasta dishes, to carry, stretch, and smooth out other flavors. We use whole-milk ricotta, but if you prefer the part-skim variety, you will find only a slight difference.

CHERRIES, DRIED

Cherries have been used in Italy since Roman times and, given the traditional methods of preservation, there may be some precedent for using dried cherries in Italian cooking. But frankly, I use dried cherries because I like the flavor, not out of any sense of tradition. We use a brand from Utah made from sour Montmorency cherries, which are naturally so tart that they are sweetened slightly before drying. Dried cherries made from sweet varieties such as Bing, Rainier, or Royal Ann are too sweet for my taste.

CHICKEN STOCK   See Stock.

CREAM

It's a popular misconception that every northern Italian dish is bathed in cream. But there are a number of dishes in which top-quality cream is essential. The kind we use is known by various names in different parts of the country (whipping cream, heavy cream, manufacturing cream); it contains pure cream, with 36 to 40 percent butterfat, and nothing else. If you have a choice, use an all-natural cream rather than one which is ultrapasteurized or has any additives. It's a good idea to buy more than a recipe calls for. One brand may not thicken exactly like another, or you may find that you don't have enough sauce after the specified amount of cream is reduced to your taste.

FOCACCIA

This flat bread, enriched with olive oil and traditionally baked directly on a stone hearth, is the original form of pizza. It's one of our most popular breads at the table, and it's also great for making Italian-style sandwiches. At Kuleto's we bake it every day. The excess never goes to waste; stale focaccia goes into soups, stuffings, even our version of crab cakes (page 52). Look for locally baked focaccia in Italian bakeries or delis, or make your own by the following recipe.

Makes one 11 × 17-inch sheet

> 5 cups bread flour, plus more for dusting
> 2 teaspoons fresh yeast (see Note)
> 2 teaspoons table salt
> 2½ tablespoons unsalted butter (room temperature)
> ¼ cup thinly sliced green onion
> 4 tablespoons (approximately) olive oil
> 2⅛ cups tepid water
> 2 teaspoons coarse sea salt or kosher salt

1. Place the flour in a large mixing bowl and crumble in the yeast. Stir in the granulated salt, butter, green onion, and 2 tablespoons of the oil. Add the water gradually and mix (with a wooden spoon, or with the dough hook if using a mixer) until the dough comes together; stop once or twice to scrape down the sides of the bowl. Knead the dough until very elastic, adding a bit more flour if the dough becomes sticky (this can take 20 minutes even with a power mixer). Form the dough into a smooth ball, place it on a lightly floured surface, cover with plastic wrap, and let rise until doubled in bulk, 1 to 1½ hours.

2. Brush the bottom and sides of an 11 × 17-inch jelly roll pan with about 1 tablespoon of oil. Punch down the dough, then flatten and stretch it with your hands into a rectangle. Transfer it to the pan and stretch it by hand to fit evenly to the edges. Cover and let the dough rise again for about 20 minutes. Meanwhile, preheat the oven to 450°F.

3. Dimple the entire top of the dough with fingertip impressions an inch or two apart. Brush lightly with oil and scatter the kosher or sea salt over the surface. Bake until golden brown, 13 to 15 minutes. If you wish, brush the top of the bread with a little more oil just after it comes out of the oven. Serve warm or at room temperature.

Variations: *Focaccia,* like pizza, lends itself to endless variations. Some are still simple breads to accompany a meal; others, especially those with cheese, can be almost a meal in themselves. Here are a few classics:

- Use 1 teaspoon chopped garlic and 2 tablespoons fresh rosemary leaves in place of the green onion.
- Use sliced shallots in place of the green onion.
- Add 2 tablespoons finely chopped fresh sage to the dough.
- Just before baking, dot the top with small chunks of Gorgonzola or Cambozola cheese. Better still, use blue cheese plus walnut pieces and slowly browned sliced onions.

Note: Denise Mondot, our pastry chef, prefers fresh (compressed) yeast to dried, and uses it in all of the 2,000 pounds of bread we bake in a typical week. Fresh yeast is sold in cakes in the refrigerator section of better supermarkets. If you have access to a commercial baker's supply, you'll find the 1-pound packages sold there are more economical and will keep well in the freezer. Fresh yeast works at lower temperatures than dry yeast, which accounts for the tepid water called for here. If you cannot find fresh yeast, use dry yeast and increase the water temperature to 100 to 110°F.

GARLIC

Look for intact, firm heads with no green sprouts showing near the top. Some times of year it seems that most of the garlic in the stores is sprouting and the flavor is especially harsh. We manage to get garlic in top condition all year, so your grocer can too. If all you can find is green and sprouting, complain to the produce buyer. Large heads generally mean fewer tiny cloves, which are a nuisance to peel.

GARLIC, ROASTED

Roasting whole heads of garlic tames the harsh flavor, transforming it into something mild and delicious. The flesh squeezes easily out of the cloves and can be used, as is or pureed, in soups or sauces, with braised meats, or simply spread on bread.

To roast garlic, choose firm, unbroken heads with no soft or sprouting cloves. Slice off enough of the tops to expose the tips of the cloves. Place the heads cut side up in a roasting pan, drizzle with a little olive oil (about a teaspoon per head), and add a sprig of thyme if desired. Cover with a lid or foil and roast in a 375°F oven until soft, golden brown, and quite fragrant, 45 minutes to an hour. Let cool, then wrap and refrigerate for up to a week.

HERBS

Several fresh herbs show up repeatedly in the recipes in this book. I like to group them into two classes, long-cooking and short-cooking herbs. The former includes rosemary, thyme, and marjoram, herbs that need some cooking time for their stronger flavors to mellow. Rosemary is important in marinades and roasted or stewed lamb, chicken, and pork. I also like the flavor it gives to a creamy, cheesy polenta (see page 113), but I rarely use it in pasta dishes. If you can't get fresh herbs, dried herbs will work for these long-cooking varieties.

Herbs such as parsley, basil (see page 20), chives, and dill work best in quicker-cooking dishes, and are typically added later in the cooking or as a garnish. I wouldn't bother with the dried version of these herbs.

MARINARA SAUCE

This most basic of Italian tomato sauces is an everday staple of our kitchen. It's occasionally used straight, but usually we combine it with other ingredients for pasta sauces.

Marinara sauce is best made with fresh tomatoes in season; when ripe fresh tomatoes are not available, a good canned tomato is preferable. A food mill is really the best tool for making this kind of pureed tomato sauce. It neatly strains out the tomato skins and seeds, rather than chopping them up as a blender or food processor does. If you don't have a food mill, be sure to use peeled tomatoes (fresh or canned), and either puree the sauce in a blender or make the chunky variation which follows.

MARINARA SAUCE I

Makes 2 cups

> 1½ cups extra virgin olive oil
> 1 cup diced onion
> 1 cup diced celery
> 1 cup diced carrot
> 2 tablespoons chopped garlic

> 2 (16-ounce) cans peeled tomatoes, drained (reserve juice) OR 2 pounds ripe tomatoes, quartered
> ¼ cup shredded basil leaves
> Salt and pepper, to taste

1. Heat the oil in a large saucepan over medium heat. Add the diced vegetables and garlic and cook until they begin to brown. Add the tomatoes and basil and cook at a simmer, stirring occasionally, until the carrots are soft, 25 to 30 minutes.

2. Put the sauce through a food mill (use the fine disc if it has interchangeable discs) and season to taste with salt and pepper. If the sauce is too thin, reduce it slightly; if too thick, thin it with a little of the reserved tomato juice.

Variation: *Marinara Sauce II (Chunky)*
Where a sauce with a chunkier texture is preferable, as in Sausage, Peppers, and Polenta (page 51) or the penne with lamb sausage on page 88, you don't have to put the sauce through a food mill. Simply cut the vegetables into very fine dice (about ⅛ inch) and chop or crush the peeled tomatoes before adding them to the pan.

MUSHROOMS

Italians are wild about mushrooms, and at various times of year the markets in Italy are full of *porcini, gallinaci, prataioli* and other delights gathered in fields and forests. The United States is beginning to catch up, and knowledgeable foragers now supply the market here with many of the same varieties and other edible fungi. Between these wild types and the increasing number of varieties now being cultivated, cooks have more mushroom choices than ever before.

Wild mushrooms deserve a cooking treatment that respects their special flavor and texture. Probably the best way to cook them is grilling over a wood or charcoal fire (see page 17), with sauteing in a little olive oil a close second. In either case, slice them at least ¼ inch thick so they keep their texture.

The king of wild mushrooms, in flavor, texture, and sometimes size, is porcini (*Boletus edulis*), with its bulbous stem and thick, meaty cap. It's found in much of North America, but especially from northern California through the Pacific Northwest. The West Coast also has several other species of *Boletus* and the closely related *Leccinum* and *Suillus* that are quite good, and we use them interchangeably.

Fresh porcini and other boletes are mostly available in the fall, but they can show up any time of year. Look for a firm cap that is moist but not slimy, greenish-yellow pores on the underside of the cap, and a heavy feel. Like some other species of mushrooms, porcini are often infested with tiny white worms (the larvae of a type of gnat) which are not always evident from the outside. The damage usually begins at the base of the stem, so the mushrooms are often sold already split in half through the stems for easy inspection. A few worm holes are not so bad, but a lot means that the stem will be soft and spongy instead of having the meaty texture typical of this species. Reject any with lots of holes throughout the stem, or, ask that the stems be removed if the caps are still sound.

The golden or orange trumpet-shaped chanterelle (*Cantharellus* spp.), known in Italy as *gallinacio*, is a little more delicate in flavor than porcini, but it's delicious in almost any mushroom presentation, from simple grilling to risotto and sauces for pasta, fish, and veal. Slices of this mushroom are as pretty to look at as they are delicious. Black chanterelles and the closely related "horn of plenty" or "trumpet of death" mushrooms are also delicious in sauces and risotto (despite the latter's scary name, it is quite edible). With either variety choose firm, dry specimens, and avoid any with soft or wet spots. (This same advice goes for most wild mushrooms.)

Fresh morels (*Morchella*) with their hollow stems and cone-shaped, wrinkled caps are hard to mistake for any other mushroom. They come out all across the country in the spring, but I find that the earliest specimens don't have as much flavor as those that appear a couple of weeks later. Look for firm, dry caps, springy but not spongy. Use them in sauces for meats or pasta, or in risotto.

Another mushroom we use frequently is a large (caps 5 to 6 inches across) brown variety with dark brown, almost black gills. I always thought this variety, known in the market as "portabella," was a wild species of *Agaricus*, the genus that includes the common commercial mushroom. It turns out it's a cultivated product, simply extra large, mature specimens of the same species (*A. bisporus*). Anyway, it's full of flavor and takes well to the same treatments as the meatier wild mushrooms. So, for that matter, do the larger sizes of commercial mushrooms.

Mushrooms of all types are very absorbent, so I try to avoid washing them if at all possible. Most commercial mushrooms are grown on sterile soil, and they are usually clean enough to use as they are. If they have a lot of debris on them, it can be brushed off or wiped off with a slightly damp towel. Use the same techniques on wild mushrooms. If there is no other way to remove dirt and debris than washing, plunge the mushrooms into water, swish them around for a few seconds, and drain immediately.

Unless one of the above varieties is specified, "mushrooms" in the recipes means the familiar commercial variety, either white or brown (the latter are sometimes labeled "crimini"). Look for unopened caps and a surface which is smooth and firm, never wet or slimy. Store all mushrooms in the refrigerator in a paper (not plastic) bag, or better still, laid out on trays lined and topped with paper towels. Wet mushrooms rot quickly. Even under the best circumstances, try to use mushrooms within a couple of days of purchase.

Caution: Gathering wild mushrooms for the table is a pleasant and time-honored practice, but if you don't know what you are doing it can be dangerous or even fatal. Some deadly poisonous varieties are difficult to distinguish from the edible ones. Responsible commercial gatherers have the training and experience to know which varieties are safe to eat, and the patience to rule out any possible confusion with dangerous varieties. The types listed above are generally safe, but some people may have individual allergic-like reactions to otherwise safe mushrooms. It's always best to try a new variety in small quantities the first time.

OIL

Most of the recipes in this book use olive oil (see below). In those cases where vegetable oil is specified, use an oil with a high smoking point, such as peanut or canola oil.

OLIVE OIL

Olive oil is practically synonymous with Italian cooking. Even in the north, where butter is the traditional cooking fat, olive oil has become essential in salad dressings, marinades, and increasingly in cooked dishes.

Two basic types of olive oil are called for in the recipes in this book. The first is extra virgin olive oil (*olio d'olive extra vergine* in Italian), a highly aromatic, greenish oil from the first cold pressing of the olive. The best of these oils come from Italy (especially Tuscany and Liguria), France, and Spain, and it's now possible to get excellent oils from California as well. At Kuleto's, we use an extra virgin oil packed to our specifications from olives grown in Orland in the Sacramento Valley.

A good extra virgin oil is full of the aroma and taste of olives. It may have a peppery aftertaste, but it should never taste harsh (some brands have a sharp, almost burning effect on the back of the throat). With a few exceptions, extra virgin oils are not used for cooking; heating them more than briefly causes most of their special aroma and flavor to evaporate.

The other type of olive oil, the one to use unless extra virgin oil is specified, is the familiar, relatively inexpensive pale and mild "pure" olive oil sold in most supermarkets and delicatessens. At Kuleto's, we use the Tiger brand from Italy sold in 3-liter cans. Other Italian brands sold in large cans, such as Bertolli, Star, and Sasso, are more or less comparable in quality, and there are also good and reasonably priced oils available from Spain and Greece. All these types are made from oils that would not qualify as extra virgin. After a refining process which removes the harsher flavors (as well as most of the desirable flavor and aroma), a small amount of extra virgin oil is added back to restore the taste and color. This type of oil is ideal for sauteing, or for dressings and marinades where the flavor of an extra virgin oil would be overpowering.

OLIVES

We use several varieties of olives at Kuleto's in everything from antipasto dishes to pastas and entrees. Most of the recipes in this book call for a particular type, such as the purplish Kalamatas from Greece, the dry-cured black "Greek" style, or Sicilian-style green olives; feel free to substitute other varieties as you like. Most varieties will benefit from a marinade like the one on page 41.

PANCETTA

Pancetta is the Italian version of bacon, cured with salt and spices (but without smoke) and typically rolled into a cylinder so the slices come out as spirals. It's used as a foundation flavor, like salt pork, usually at the beginning of cooking a soup or sauce. We use it in bean soups (see page 66), and certain pasta dishes (especially those with clams and other shellfish).

Most recipes call for sliced pancetta, but it keeps better in unsliced form. Unless you have a source where you can buy it easily, it's best to buy a larger chunk and slice it off as you need it. Well wrapped, a chunk of pancetta will keep for a couple of weeks in the refrigerator.

PESTO

This puree of basil, garlic, olive oil, and grated cheese is best known as a sauce for pasta, but it is much more versatile than that. A dab of pesto is a handy way of adding fresh basil flavor to other sauces and salad dressings, and it makes a great alternative to tomato sauce as a pizza topping. Make a batch whenever fresh basil is cheap, freeze it in ice cube trays, and you will have a ready supply of 2-tablespoon portions of pesto on hand.

PESTO

Makes a scant 2 cups

>   1 cup extra virgin olive oil
>   6 large cloves garlic
> ⅓ cup toasted pine nuts
> ¼ cup grated Parmesan cheese
>   4 cups (loosely packed) fresh basil leaves
>   (about 2 good-sized summer bunches)
> ½ teaspoon salt
>   Pinch of pepper

Combine all the ingredients in a blender and blend to a smooth paste (a long-handled ladle of at least 4 ounces capacity makes a good tool for pushing the leaves down into the blender jar without the risk of getting caught in the blades). Taste for seasoning and adjust if necessary. Store tightly covered, ideally with plastic wrap pressed down against the surface to prevent air from darkening the pesto.

When pesto stands for a while, the green-stained oil seeps out and sits on top. If you make pesto in quantity, you may have a fair amount of this oil, which is as flavorful as it is colorful. A bit of pesto-flavored oil can be just the thing to garnish an entree, pasta, or risotto (see Risotto with Spring Vegetables, page 96).

POLENTA

Coarsely ground yellow cornmeal, as well as the dish made from it (see page 112).

PROSCIUTTO

This firm, dry-cured, unsmoked ham, aged for a minimum of 9 months and often for a year or more, is one of the essential flavors of Italian cuisine. It is definitely salty, but in a good prosciutto the salty flavor is in balance with the natural sweet flavor of the pork.

Served raw, prosciutto is often paired with fruit. Melon and figs are the most traditional partners, but it also goes well with peaches, grapes, and other sweet fruit. As an ingredient in cooked dishes, prosciutto adds both its salty ham flavor and a bit of texture to dishes such as the ricotta stuffing in the chicken breasts on page 122 and various pasta dishes. Unlike pancetta, which usually goes into the dish at the beginning of cooking, I tend to add prosciutto toward the end of the cooking, so it just begins to release its flavor. We've even used crisp-fried strips of prosciutto as a garnish for fish dishes.

We use imported Italian *prosciutto di Parma*, but the hams from Siena and San Daniele are also very good. There are a couple of North American brands that stand out from the rest, including Fiorucci from Virginia and Volpi from St. Louis. I don't recommend the domestic versions sold under big national brands—most are too salty for my taste. When shopping for prosciutto, don't be afraid to ask for a taste and compare brands. Look for a nice pink color to the meat, rather than a deeper red, and fat that is pure white, not yellowing.

Store sliced prosciutto tightly wrapped, preferably in single layers on waxed paper (it should come this way from better delis). If you are confident in your knife skills, you might want to buy prosciutto in larger pieces and slice it as you need it. If well wrapped, large pieces will keep for weeks in the refrigerator.

RADICCHIO

The Italian word *radicchio* covers a number of related varieties of red-leafed chicory, of which the best known is the round, red and white *radicchio di Verona*. The other major variety is the slender, pointed *radicchio di Treviso*, which is shaped rather like large Belgian endive. Unless otherwise specified in the recipes, use the Verona variety; if you can't get either, Belgian endive gives a bit of the same flavor, though not the color.

Unknown until recently in this country, imported radicchio is now fairly easy to find in well-stocked produce markets in the bigger cities, and it is also being grown in California and the Northwest, and perhaps in other parts of the country by now. So far I haven't tasted a domestic radicchio that measures up to the Italian version; the imported has tighter heads, the taste is less bitter, and it holds its bright red color better. But the quality of the local version seems to get better each year. If you have a garden you might try growing your own; seeds are available from a number of speciality seed catalogs.

Raw radicchio leaves give color and a nice touch of bitterness to mixed green salads. Cooking tones down the bitterness, emphasizing a nutty flavor that enhances sauces for pasta and seafood, especially those made with cream. But the most popular use for radicchio at Kuleto's is quartered whole heads wrapped in pancetta and grilled (see page 50).

SAUSAGE

Several recipes in this book call for an uncooked Italian-style sausage made of ground pork with various spices, of which fennel seed is prominent. This kind of sausage is available just about everywhere, usually in two versions—hot, with red pepper, and mild or "sweet," without. If you have access to a meat grinder, you might prefer to make your own. It's a bit cheaper to buy the plain pork and season, grind, and stuff it yourself, but the main advantage is that you can vary the seasonings to suit your own tastes. The following recipe, for example, is on the hot side with red pepper flakes and cayenne; if you prefer a milder sausage, you can cut down or eliminate the red pepper. (Don't, however, cut down on the salt, which is necessary to preserve the meat.)

Lamb sausages are not common in Italy, but I have included a recipe for one below because it is used in one of our more popular dishes, the penne with sausage and chard on page 88.

Whether homemade or bought, fresh sausage will keep in the refrigerator for up to 3 days; for longer storage, wrap it tightly and store in the freezer for up to 6 months. For convenience in thawing only what you need, pack it in 1-pound batches or whatever size is appropriate.

FRESH ITALIAN SAUSAGE

Makes 5 pounds (about 20 sausages)

>   Medium hog casings (available
>   from specialty butchers)
>   1 heaping tablespoon fennel seed
>   1 teaspoon black peppercorns
>   2 teaspoons coriander seed
>   3 tablespoons kosher salt OR 2 table-
>   spoons granulated salt
>   1 heaping teaspoon sugar
>   1½ teaspoons red pepper flakes

>   1 teaspoon cayenne
>   1 teaspoon ground nutmeg
>   1 tablespoon paprika
>   5 pounds boneless pork butt (see Note)
>   1 heaping teaspoon minced garlic
>   2 tablespoons ice water

1. Soak about a 12-foot length of casings in water for 30 minutes, then rinse by running cold tap water through them. Grind the fennel seed, peppercorns, and coriander seed and combine them with the salt, sugar, and remaining spices. Separate the meat along the natural seams and remove any gristle. Cut the meat and fat into strips of any length, but narrow enough to fit into the entry chute of your grinder. Grind half the meat and fat together through the coarse plate (⅜-inch holes), then the remainder through the fine plate (⅛- to ³⁄₁₆-inch). Combine the two grinds in a large mixing bowl and add the seasonings, garlic, and water. Mix with the paddle attachment on an electric mixer or knead by hand until the seasonings are evenly spread throughout the meat.

2. Remove the cutting blade from the grinder and fit on the sausage-stuffing horn. Slide the full length of the casing onto the horn. Pack the sausage mixture into the grinder and turn the crank until sausage begins to come out of the end of the horn. Stop and pull off a short length of casing, tie an overhand knot in the end, and continue cranking to fill the casing. Let the finished sausage fall in loose coils on the counter. If the casing tears or a hole appears, stop stuffing, cut off and tie off the finished section, and begin with a new knotted end.

3. If you want to form the sausage into links, pinch the casing in 5-inch lengths and give every other section two or three twists.

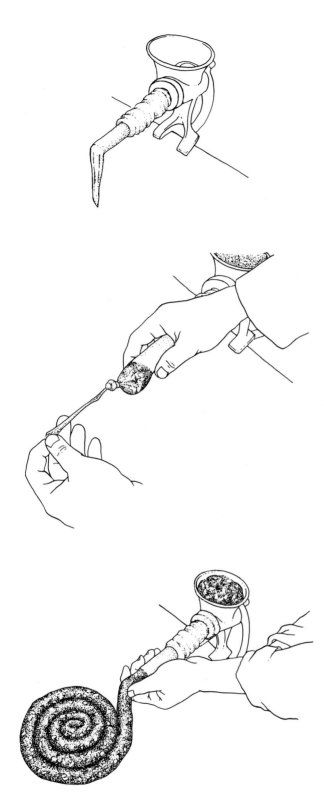

Note: Pork "butt," actually a cut from the shoulder, contains just about the right proportion of fat for a moist sausage in its usual retail trim, that is, with the outer layer of fat trimmed to about a ¼-inch layer. Ask if your butcher or market will sell you the whole butt at a special price; at 7 to 8 pounds, with only a piece of shoulder blade to bone out, it should yield enough for this recipe and an extra couple of pounds of meat and cost about what 5 pounds of boned and cut-up shoulder would sell for in the retail case.

LAMB SAUSAGE

Makes 5 pounds

> 4½ pounds boneless lamb shoulder
> 1 pound salt pork, diced
> 1 tablespoon cumin
> 4 tablespoons fennel seed
> 1½ teaspoons minced fresh ginger
> 1½ tablespoons minced garlic
> 1 tablespoon red pepper flakes

1. Remove and discard all the visible fat from the lamb. Cut the meat into 2-inch cubes and combine it with the salt pork in a large bowl. Grind the cumin and fennel, mix them with the other seasonings, and sprinkle over the meat. Toss to coat evenly, cover, and let stand overnight in the refrigerator.

2. Grind the meat mixture once through the fine plate of a meat grinder. The sausage is now ready for forming into patties, or it can be stuffed into casings like Fresh Italian Sausage, above.

Note: It is no mistake that there is no salt in this recipe; the salt pork provides plenty.

Top to bottom: The empty casing on the stuffing horn; tying off the end; stuffing and coiling the sausage.

STOCK

Two stocks are used throughout this book, a pale chicken stock and a light brown veal stock. The former is our equivalent of the typical light, clear Italian *brodo* or meat broth, and we use it to make most of our soups and risotti, as well as some pasta sauces. This is such a simple and economical stock to make that I can't imagine being without it. If you make a habit of buying whole chickens rather than parts and save the backs, necks, wingtips, and miscellaneous bones and trimmings, you'll find it easy to maintain a steady supply of chicken stock in your refrigerator or freezer.

A light stock is the only one made in most Italian homes. But there are times, especially in making sauces, when we want the richer flavor and additional body of a brown veal stock in the French style. This stock is admittedly more trouble to make, not to mention more expensive, but I think it's worth it on both counts. And if using a meaty cut of veal like the breast just for making stock seems extravagant, you can use the cooked meat in pasta sauces or stuffings, or serve it hot or cold as plain boiled meat.

Both of the following stocks will keep well in the refrigerator if brought to a boil every three or four days. They will keep for months in the freezer.

CHICKEN STOCK

Makes about 3 quarts

> 3 pounds chicken backs, necks, trimmings, and giblets (not livers)
> 1 large onion, peeled and chopped
> 1 cup chopped carrot
> 1 cup chopped celery
> 1 bay leaf
> 1 sprig fresh thyme

Rinse the chicken pieces and place them in a large pot with the vegetables. Add cold water to cover and bring to a boil; once the stock begins to boil, skim off the foam that rises to the surface. Reduce the heat to low, add the herbs, and simmer uncovered 2 to 3 hours. (It should taste and smell like good chicken stock at this point; if not, cook it longer.) Strain and refrigerate the stock until ready to use. Discard the fat from the top before using.

BROWN VEAL STOCK

Makes about 4 quarts

> 2 to 3 pounds breast of veal (3 ribs)
> 3 pounds veal bones, sliced with a saw or cracked
> 1 pound onions, peeled and quartered
> ½ pound carrots, scrubbed and cut into 2-inch lengths
> ½ pound celery, cut in 2-inch lengths
> 1½ cups red wine
> 1 head garlic, halved crosswise
> 1 or 2 bay leaves
> 1 teaspoon whole peppercorns

1. Preheat the oven to 400°F. Separate the veal breast into ribs, then chop each rib crosswise with a cleaver into 3 or 4 sections. (Or ask the butcher to cut across the ribs with a band saw every 2 inches, then cut between the ribs.) Place the ribs and bones in a large roasting pan and roast until the meat begins to brown, about 20 minutes. Add the vegetables and continue roasting until they are nicely browned, another 30 to 40 minutes.

2. Transfer the contents of the roasting pan to a stockpot. Pour the wine into the roasting pan, scrape up any browned bits from the pan, and add the mixture to the stockpot. Add cold water to cover, bring to a boil, and skim off any foam

that comes to the surface. Reduce the heat to the lowest your stove will maintain, add the garlic, bay leaves, and peppercorns and simmer uncovered 6 to 8 hours. Strain and refrigerate until ready to use. Discard the fat from the top before using.

Note: If you want to rescue some of the meat for another purpose, pull the meaty rib pieces out of the stock halfway through the simmering time. When cool enough to handle, pull off the meat. Return the bones and trimmings to the pot.

TOMATOES

Our customers expect us to have fresh tomatoes all year, and in some months we really have to lean on our purveyors and pay exorbitant prices to find the best tomatoes available. Still, tomatoes never taste as good as when they are locally grown in season. In the recipes that call for cooking tomatoes, you're better off using a good canned tomato whenever fresh locally grown tomatoes are unavailable.

To peel, seed, and chop fresh tomatoes, slash the skins with a shallow X, plunge them into boiling water for 30 seconds or so, then transfer them to a bowl of cold water to cool. The skins should slip off easily. Slice the tomatoes in half crosswise and gently squeeze out the seeds, then chop the flesh to the desired size.

TOMATOES, SUN-DRIED

Before the invention of canning, the only way to preserve tomatoes was to dry them in the sun, the same process that turns fresh grapes into raisins and plums into prunes. Like other dried fruit, dried tomatoes would keep long after the fresh tomato season was over, and were the only form of tomatoes available through the winter and spring. Italians would probably be surprised at how popular dried tomatoes have become with Americans in recent years, even at times of year when fresh tomatoes are available. But fresh and dried tomatoes have such different flavors and textures (like fresh grapes and raisins) that it makes sense to me to treat them as totally different ingredients. We take advantage of the sweet, concentrated flavor and slightly chewy texture of dried tomatoes in pastas, sauces, and vegetable garnishes for meats and poultry.

Dried tomatoes are available in two forms, dry and packed in oil. The former are less expensive, but have to be reconstituted with water before they are edible; the latter have been reconstituted already before they are stored in oil. We buy the dry version (a California brand, sold in bulk) and reconstitute a batch of them every other day as follows: Heat about ¼ inch of water in a skillet, add the tomatoes, cover, and steam over low heat, shaking or stirring to moisten them evenly, until the tomatoes are plump and tender, 2 to 3 minutes. Remove and let drain on a cooling rack. The tomatoes are now ready to use, and will keep for a day or two in the refrigerator. To keep them longer, pack them into clean jars and add olive oil to cover them completely; they will keep indefinitely in the refrigerator. (Once you have used the tomatoes, the flavored oil can be used in dressings and marinades.)

VEAL STOCK See Stock.

VINEGAR

Any alcoholic beverage can be the base for vinegar (the product of bacterial action which converts the alcohol into acetic acid), but the only vinegars that give an authentic Italian flavor are made from wine. The type of wine determines the color, flavor, and uses of the vinegar. *White wine vinegar,* often labeled Champagne vinegar, is pale and rather delicate in flavor; we use it mainly when a darker vinegar would discolor pale ingredients, as in the Tuscan Bread Salad on page 125. Otherwise, we use a *red wine vinegar,* which has a slightly fuller flavor and a deeper color.

Balsamic vinegar is a very special form of vinegar from Modena, Italy. This dark brown, smooth, and slightly sweet vinegar full of complex flavors and aromas is made by boiling down the juice of Trebbiano grapes prior to fermentation and aging the vinegar for many years in a series of 12 barrels, each made of a different wood. It's actually higher in acidity than other wine vinegars (6 percent versus 5 percent), but the acidity is balanced by the other flavors.

Like sun-dried tomatoes and arugula, balsamic vinegar has become very popular with Americans in recent years; to a traditional Modenese point of view we probably use it to excess. It certainly makes a delicious vinaigrette (see Mixed Greens with Balsamic Vinaigrette, page 102), but its character is so distinctive that it may not appeal to everyone. Don't assume that anything made with red wine vinegar would be better if made with balsamic. They are two completely different ingredients.

The finest balsamic vinegars, some of which are aged for 50 years or more, are almost as smooth as liqueurs, and are used in tiny quantities for special purposes, such as dressing strawberries. However, most of the balsamic vinegar sold in the U.S. is much younger, and made by a faster process. In Italy, the younger version is officially known as *aceto balsamico industriale,* to distinguish it from the traditional *aceto balsamico naturale* described above. We use the younger type in our vinaigrette, but feel free to use the more expensive older versions if your budget allows. Even with the less expensive "industrial" type, brands of balsamic vinegar vary widely in quality; some are much harsher than others. As with any other ingredient, taste different brands and see which ones you prefer.

WINES FOR COOKING

Several recipes in the book call for a small amount of wine as a cooking liquid. It should go without saying that the wines you choose to cook with should be good enough to drink; cooking down a bad wine simply concentrates its faults. When a recipe calls for a dry white wine, choose an inexpensive but pleasant white with good acidity and no dominant flavors of oak or exotic fruit. There are plenty of good examples of this type from California, Italy, Australia, and Chile.

Some dishes made with red wine, particularly Osso Buco (page 130), get a large part of their flavor from the wine, so it's important to choose it carefully. If the wine tastes excessively grapey or raisiny (as some inexpensive wines can), or tastes like it's beginning to turn to vinegar, so will the sauce. On the other hand, there is no need to use an expensive aged wine; just look for an inexpensive red which has had some aging, either before bottling or in the bottle. Sometimes an older red in which the fruit is beginning to fade can be a perfect choice for cooking. A good wine merchant should be able to suggest a few reasonably priced red and white wines for cooking.

APPETIZERS

— ANTIPASTI —

Marinated Olives

Marinated Artichokes

Marinated Grilled Mushrooms

Grilled Eggplant and Tomato Salad with Fresh Mozzarella

Calamari Salad

Grilled Wild Mushrooms with Polenta and Cambozola

Grilled Radicchio Wrapped in Pancetta

Sausage, Peppers, and Polenta

Focaccia Crab Cakes

Orange and Herb-Cured Salmon

Deep-Fried Squid

Cheese-Flavored Breadsticks

Grilled Garlic Bread with Tomatoes

Grilled Stuffed Figs or Apricots

Somewhere near the front door of most restaurants in Italy is a table of marinated vegetables, salads, cured meats, and olives, designed to tempt the diner with a little something to precede the items on the menu. Collectively, these tidbits are known as antipasto, which literally means "before the meal" (not "before the pasta," as it is often mistranslated).

A good antipasto is an "appetizer" in the truest sense, something flavorful and a bit dramatic to wake up the taste buds. It can be as modest as a few thin slices of prosciutto with figs or pieces of melon, or as substantial as a small plate of sausage with peppers and polenta. In general, this is not stand-up cocktail party food, but little dishes meant to be eaten at the table, with knife and fork.

Not every meal needs an antipasto; it's most appropriate for entertaining, when you are taking your time, relaxing with friends and family, and making an evening of a meal and good conversation. When I'm entertaining at home, the antipasto course often takes as much time as the rest of the meal. If the main course features something from the grill, the perfect antipasto might be an assortment of grilled vegetables, served with sliced tomatoes, fresh mozzarella or perhaps a bit of a richer cheese like Cambozola, and toasted focaccia. For a more dramatic starter, wrap quartered radicchio heads with pancetta, grill them, and serve with a pesto-flavored dressing.

In a more formal meal, consider starting with a plate of *antipasto misto*: an assortment of marinated vegetables, perhaps some slices of prosciutto or excellent salami or coppa, and some crisp *grissini* (breadsticks). A mixed antipasto plate can be varied with whatever you have on hand — leftover cooked vegetables or fish, roasted potatoes, even canned tuna or sardines — dressed with a little vinaigrette.

MARINATED OLIVES

Olives are delicious straight from the jar, but they get even better when dressed with oil, vinegar, garlic, and an assortment of Mediterranean herbs. At Kuleto's, we use these marinated olives in lots of ways—on antipasto plates, in salads, and as a garnish in cooked dishes. They will keep almost indefinitely in the refrigerator, so long as you toss them now and then to keep them all moist. Once the olives are gone, strain the marinade and use it for a salad dressing.

Makes 3 cups

> 1½ pounds (drained weight) assorted olives (see Note)
> 1 or 2 sprigs *each* fresh thyme, sage, rosemary, and oregano or marjoram
> 2 bay leaves

3 cloves garlic, sliced
Olive oil
Red wine vinegar

Combine the olives, herbs, and garlic in a glass or stainless steel container. Add enough olive oil and vinegar (3 parts olive oil to 1 part vinegar) to cover them at least halfway. Cover and refrigerate at least overnight, stirring once or twice. When serving, use a slotted spoon and try to get olives from the bottom, where they have had the most contact with the marinade.

Note: This recipe will work with any variety of full-flavored olive or, better still, a blend of varieties. We combine the purplish Kalamatas, the dry-cured black "Greek" style, and a Sicilian-style green olive that we cure ourselves using locally grown Sevillano olives.

MARINATED ARTICHOKES

Like the olives on page 41, these can show up in various courses, from antipasto dishes to pastas and entrees. If you live where fresh artichokes are available at a reasonable price, you may never buy the bottled version again.

Makes about 36 halves

> 1 tablespoon vinegar or lemon juice
> 2 pounds small artichokes (see Note)
>   Juice of 1 large or 2 small lemons
> 1 bay leaf
> 1 sprig fresh thyme
> ½ teaspoon peppercorns
> ⅓ cup Balsamic Vinaigrette (see page 103)

1. Fill a medium bowl with water and add the tablespoon of vinegar or lemon juice to acidulate it. Peel off the outer leaves from the artichokes until you reach leaves that are more yellow than green. Trim the stems with a knife, removing any traces of dark green outer skin. Slice off the top of each artichoke, about a third of the way down the leaves. If the artichokes are on the large side, slice them in half; otherwise leave them whole. As you finish trimming each artichoke, drop it into the bowl of acidulated water.

2. Drain the artichokes and place them in a nonreactive saucepan. Add the lemon juice, herbs, peppercorns, and water to cover. Place a small heatproof plate, the lid from a smaller pan, or some other weight on top of the artichokes to keep them submerged. Bring to a boil, reduce the heat, and simmer until the artichokes are tender, 35 to 40 minutes. Drain.

3. Toss the warm artichokes in the vinaigrette and let them stand at least 2 hours before serving, or refrigerate for up to 3 days.

Note: Sometimes called "baby" artichokes or artichoke "hearts," these small (about the size of an egg) artichokes are sold by weight, not by the piece. At this size, they have not developed the inedible fuzzy choke in the center, so once the outside leaves are trimmed the entire artichoke is edible.

Variation: Cooked but not marinated artichokes (prepared through step 2) are a versatile ingredient in many dishes. We frequently use them cut into quarters or wedges in pasta sauces, along with mushrooms or other vegetables. Or try them as the vegetable accompaniment to Osso Buco (page 130) or other braised meats.

MARINATED GRILLED
MUSHROOMS

Grilling over a wood or charcoal fire gives extra aroma and flavor to ordinary mushrooms, but even if cooked in a skillet (see Variation), these marinated mushroom caps are a fine addition to a mixed antipasto platter. Sliced, they add a nice meaty texture to salads such as the spinach salad on page 106. Fresh shiitake mushrooms, though not very Italian, are especially good this way. Ignore the part about unopened caps with shiitakes—the caps are always open in this species.

Makes about 24

> 1 pound medium mushrooms, with caps unopened
> ¼ cup extra virgin olive oil
> Salt and freshly ground pepper to taste
> 2 tablespoons balsamic vinegar

Brush the mushrooms clean or, if they are very dirty, wash them quickly and drain well. Pull off the stems (slice them off if using shiitakes); discard the stems or save them for the stock pot. Toss the caps with the olive oil and a bit of salt and pepper. Grill them over a medium-hot fire until nicely browned, 2 to 3 minutes per side, then return them to the bowl. Toss with the vinegar and additional salt and pepper, if needed. Let cool to room temperature before serving.

Variation: If grilling is not practical, cook the mushroom caps in a very lightly oiled skillet over high heat until they begin to release their moisture, 4 to 7 minutes depending on size. (You probably won't be able to cook them all at once; start with as many as will fit in a single layer, and either cook them in batches or add more to the pan as they shrink and space becomes available.) Finish cooking the mushrooms with the gill side down so they steam slightly in the released moisture.

Marinated Artichokes and Marinated Grilled Mushrooms

GRILLED
EGGPLANT AND TOMATO
SALAD WITH
FRESH MOZZARELLA

This salad is the essence of late summer—ripe eggplant, tomatoes, and sweet basil combined with the delicate flavor of fresh mozzarella. Grilling brings out the flavor of eggplant like no other cooking method, so I recommend throwing some on the grill whenever you have the fire going, whether you will serve it at the same meal or not. This salad works equally well with still-warm eggplant grilled on the same fire as the entree or leftover grilled slices from the previous day.

Serves 4 to 6

> 1 small eggplant (about ¾ pound)
> Salt and freshly ground pepper
> Olive oil, for brushing
> 2 large tomatoes, sliced
> 12 small balls (*bocconcini*) or 12 1-ounce slices fresh mozzarella (room temperature)
> ½ cup Balsamic Vinaigrette (see page 103)
> Fresh basil leaves, for garnish

1. Split the eggplant lengthwise and cut each half crosswise into six equal slices, about ¾ inch thick. Season the slices lightly with salt and pepper and brush with a little oil. Grill over a moderately hot fire until tender and lightly browned, 4 to 5 minutes per side. If not serving immediately, set aside.

2. Arrange a layer of eggplant on a platter or individual plates. Top with a layer of tomatoes and arrange the mozzarella pieces on top. Drizzle the dressing over all and garnish generously with basil.

CALAMARI SALAD

At about a dollar a pound, squid (calamari) has to be the best bargain in seafood, and a perfect addition to a salad. Just be sure you don't over-cook the squid; as soon as it turns opaque it is done, and after that it only gets tougher. Vary the vegetables and garnishes with capers, sweet peppers, sliced fennel, or basil leaves. For a hot-ter flavor, add some red pepper flakes to the dressing.

Serves 4 to 6

> 1½ pounds whole squid OR 1 pound cleaned squid
> ½ large red onion (halved through the root end), peeled
> ½ large rib celery
> 2 ripe Roma tomatoes
>
> **DRESSING**
> 1 clove garlic, minced and mashed
> 2 tablespoons lime or lemon juice
> ¾ teaspoon kosher salt
> ¼ teaspoon freshly ground pepper
> 3 tablespoons olive oil
> 2 tablespoons chopped parsley

1. Clean the squid (see Note, page 55), leaving the tentacles in clusters. Peel the spotted outer skin from the sacs and cut the sacs into rings. Rinse well and drain. Bring a pot of lightly salted water to a boil, and have a bowl of ice water at hand. Add the squid to the pot and cook just until the tentacles curl back and the rings become opaque white, about 30 seconds. Drain and trans-fer the squid to the ice-water bowl to stop the cooking. Drain well.

2. Split the onion half through the root end, then cut each quarter crosswise into thin slices. Split the celery lengthwise and cut it into thin diagonal slices. Halve the tomatoes lengthwise, remove the cores, and slice the flesh lengthwise. Combine the vegetables in a bowl with the cooked squid. Mix the dressing ingredients thoroughly, pour it over the salad, and toss to coat evenly. Refrigerate 1 to 4 hours for the flavors to blend; remove from the refrigerator 30 minutes or so before serving.

GRILLED WILD MUSHROOMS
WITH POLENTA
AND CAMBOZOLA

When you can find big, meaty wild mushrooms in the market (or in the woods, if you know what you are doing), I know of no better way to prepare them than to grill them in thick slices, preferably over a wood fire. (See page 27 for a discussion of the various types of mushrooms appropriate to this dish.) To make a good thing even better, serve them with a *fonduta*, a rich, creamy cheese sauce. The sauce is so good, you might want to serve it over polenta even without the mushrooms.

Serves 4

FONDUTA DI CAMBOZOLA
½ head roasted garlic (see page 25),
    peeled and mashed
5 ounces Cambozola cheese
½ cup whipping cream

———

4 triangles polenta, prepared for grilling
    as described on page 112
Olive oil
Salt and freshly ground pepper
½ pound porcini, chanterelles, or other
    meaty wild mushrooms, cleaned
    and sliced at least ¼ inch thick
2 teaspoons chopped chives

1. Prepare a medium-hot fire in an open or covered grill. If you do not already have some roasted garlic on hand, place a whole head near the edge of the heat while the fire is getting ready for cooking. Roast until the outer cloves are quite soft. Let it cool enough to handle then slice it in half crosswise, squeeze out half of the cloves, and mash them with a fork.

2. For the *fonduta*, scrape the white rind off the cheese and cut the cheese into small cubes. Whisk the cream and garlic together in a skillet over medium heat; bring just to a boil, reduce slightly, and stir in the cheese a little at a time, whisking until smooth. Keep warm.

3. Brush the polenta pieces with a little oil and season with salt and pepper. Grill, starting with the bumpy side down, until heated through and lightly browned, about 3 minutes per side. As they are done, move them to the edge of the grill to keep warm, or to warmed plates. Oil and season the mushroom slices and grill them over the hottest part of the fire until tender and nicely browned, 2 to 4 minutes per side. To serve, place a piece of polenta on each plate, arrange mushroom slices on top, and spoon the fonduta over all. Garnish with chives.

Variation: This also works well with extra-large cultivated mushrooms, including "portabella," oyster mushrooms, and fresh shiitakes. Leave the latter two whole if on the small side, or split them in half lengthwise if larger, but don't try to cut the caps into slices or they will be too small.

GRILLED RADICCHIO
WRAPPED IN PANCETTA

A dramatic but balanced combination of strong flavors and textures has made this one of the signature dishes at Kuleto's. Cooking radicchio tones down its bitter flavor, but it's still bitter enough to balance the peppery-sweet-salty pancetta, the tangy vinaigrette and goat cheese garnish, and the richness of the pesto-flavored dressing.

Serves 4

> ¼ cup Caesar Dressing (see page 105)
> 1 tablespoon Pesto (see page 29)
> 1 large head red radicchio (6 to 8 ounces)
> 4 thin slices pancetta
> ¼ cup Balsamic Vinaigrette (see page 103)
> 1 ounce fresh goat cheese, crumbled

1. Combine the Caesar dressing and pesto and blend thoroughly. Remove any damaged outer leaves from the radicchio and trim any excess from the base. Cut the head into quarters lengthwise. Wrap each quarter in a slice of pancetta and secure the ends with a toothpick. Drizzle each piece with the balsamic vinaigrette, letting it run down between the leaves. Grill over a moderately hot fire until well browned on all sides, about 10 minutes in all.

2. During the last 2 minutes or so of cooking, remove the toothpicks, turn the radicchio bundles cut sides up, and baste with about 2 tablespoons of the pesto dressing. Continue cooking until the surface is slightly glazed.

3. Spread the remaining pesto dressing on a large plate. Arrange the radicchio bundles on top, and scatter goat cheese over all. Serve immediately.

Variation: If radicchio is unavailable, substitute 2 heads of Belgian endive, split lengthwise. Because its flavor is milder, Belgian endive needs less cooking. Use the hottest part of the fire and cut the grilling time in half, or grill just until the pancetta is well browned.

SAUSAGE, PEPPERS, AND POLENTA

This is a pretty substantial dish as antipasti go. Plan to follow it with a light entree, or perhaps serve a seafood pasta or risotto and skip the entree. The quantity here would also do nicely as a lunch or supper entree for two, with just a salad.

Serves 4

> 2 (4-inch) squares polenta, cooked and cooled as for Grilled Polenta (see page 112)
> 3 tablespoons olive oil
> 2 (4-ounce) Italian sausages, sliced into ¼-inch rounds and blanched
> 1 teaspoon minced garlic
> ½ cup sliced roasted and peeled sweet pepper (about 1 large pepper)
> 1 cup Marinara Sauce (see page 26)
> ½ cup grated aged Provolone or Cacciocavallo cheese

1. Preheat the oven to 450°F, or set an oven rack 3 to 4 inches below the broiler. Cut the polenta squares in half to make 4 triangles. Arrange them in a row on a heatproof oval platter or put them on 4 individual heatproof plates. Brush with a little of the oil and bake or broil until lightly browned, about 3 minutes.

2. Meanwhile, heat the remaining oil in a skillet over medium-high heat. Add the sliced sausages, garlic, and pepper and cook until the sausages are cooked through (break a slice open to check the inside). Stir in the marinara sauce and cook just until heated through.

3. Spoon the sausage mixture over the polenta, top with the grated cheese, and return to the oven until the cheese melts.

FOCACCIA
CRAB CAKES

This is an Italian kitchen's version of the all-American crab cake. I like the texture that irregular pieces of focaccia give better than the more usual bread crumbs. It's important to use fresh, not stale, focaccia or the cakes may be too dry.

This recipe makes 15 to 16 cakes. In the restaurant we serve three on a plate, but you might find two enough as a first course.

Serves 5 to 8

> 3 tablespoons olive oil
> 1 tablespoon butter
> ½ cup *each* finely diced celery, onion, and red bell pepper
> 1 teaspoon minced garlic
> 2 cups diced (¼-inch cubes) fresh Focaccia (see page 22), homemade or bought
> 1 pound cooked crab meat
> 2 large eggs
> 1 teaspoon celery salt
> ½ teaspoon paprika
> ¼ teaspoon cayenne
> 1 teaspoon Worcestershire sauce
> ½ cup Basil Aioli (see page 18)
> Fresh basil leaves, for garnish

1. Heat 1 tablespoon of the oil and the butter in a skillet and cook the diced vegetables and garlic until soft but not browned. Transfer the mixture to a bowl and combine it with the bread cubes.

2. Pick over the crab meat to remove any bits of shell. Add the crab to the bowl. Toss by hand, breaking up the crab and bread slightly.

3. Beat the eggs lightly with the remaining seasonings and add them to the bowl. Stir until well blended and set aside to rest 1 to 2 hours.

4. Form the crab mixture firmly into mounds about the size of a golf ball (a small ice cream scoop is ideal for making nice tight cakes with no air pockets). The cakes should be nearly as tall as they are wide, because they will flatten somewhat in cooking.

5. Heat the remaining oil in a large skillet over medium-high heat. Add as many of the cakes as will fit without crowding and cook until nicely browned on the bottom. Flatten the tops slightly with a spatula, then turn and cook them until browned on the other side and heated through. Serve with Basil Aioli and garnish with basil leaves.

Variation: If you prefer cakes with a crisper coating, roll them in fine dried bread crumbs before cooking. The same soft focaccia crumbs used in the cakes won't work.

ORANGE AND HERB-CURED SALMON

This Italian take on the Scandinavian *gravlax* uses Mediterranean herbs and orange peel in place of the usual dill, but the basic curing method is the same. A mixture of salt and sugar draws excess moisture out of the fish, giving it a texture like that of cold-smoked salmon.

The recipe makes enough salmon for 8 to 12 servings, more than you need for this dish, but leftovers will keep for at least a week and it really doesn't make sense to cure less than a pound. Of course, you can expand the recipe for a larger piece of fish, anywhere up to a whole side of salmon. Note that the curing takes 2 days.

Serves 4 to 6

> 1 pound skin-on salmon filet (see Note)
> 1 cup sugar
> 1 cup kosher salt
> 2 medium oranges
> 1 large bunch fresh oregano, marjoram, or basil, or a blend, roughly chopped (about ½ cup chopped)
> 1 medium fennel bulb, sliced crosswise as thinly as possible
> ½ medium red onion, sliced crosswise as thinly as possible
> 2 teaspoons champagne vinegar
> 1½ tablespoons extra virgin olive oil
> Salt and red pepper flakes or cayenne, to taste

1. Remove any pin bones from the salmon filet with tweezers or clean needle-nosed pliers. Combine the sugar and salt. Spread a piece of perforated foil or cheesecloth large enough to wrap the fish in the bottom of a stainless or glass baking pan. Spread half the sugar and salt mixture in the center to match the outlines of the fish. Lay the fish on top. Zest 1 of the oranges and cover the fish with an even layer of grated zest. Add a layer of herbs, then spread the remaining sugar and salt on top. Wrap the foil or cheesecloth around the fish and secure the ends. Place another rigid pan on top of the fish and weight it down with 2 to 4 pounds (a couple of quart jars, several cans of food, a half gallon of milk, or something similar) on top. Refrigerate for 2 days. Drain off the accumulated liquid once or twice beginning the second day.

2. After 2 days, remove the weight and drain off all the liquid from the pan. Brush off any remaining salt and sugar (it may have all dissolved), but leave the layer of herbs intact if possible. Pat the fish dry.

3. Slice the tops and bottoms off the oranges. With a sharp knife, cut away the peel and white pith and the thin membranes on the outside of each section. Working over a bowl to catch the juice, cut the sections away from the inner membranes dividing them. Put the orange sections in the bowl and squeeze in the juice from the cores.

4. To serve, slice the salmon thinly on a diagonal, catching a bit of the herb coating on each slice. Arrange 3 or 4 slices around the edge of each chilled dinner plate. Drain off and reserve the juice from the oranges. Add the fennel and onions to the orange sections. Combine the orange juice, vinegar, oil, salt, and red pepper and whisk to blend. Add the mixture to the salad bowl, toss to coat, then place a small pile of the salad in the center of each plate.

Note: Use the freshest, highest quality salmon you can find. My choices would be king salmon from the Pacific Northwest or farm-raised Atlantic salmon, which can come from Norway, Canada, or Puget Sound.

DEEP-FRIED SQUID

I can sympathize with those who have never tried squid; after all, it was hardly one of the basic food resources of Fort Wayne, Indiana, where I grew up. Frankly, it took me a while to learn to like it, but now I love it. I think this recipe is the ideal introduction to this cheap, abundant, and delicious mollusk.

If you have a choice, fresh squid comes out a bit more tender than frozen, but frozen is still fine as long as you don't overcook it.

Serves 2

> ½ pound whole squid OR 5 to 6 ounces cleaned squid, including tentacles
> Oil for deep-frying
> 1 teaspoon Worcestershire sauce
> Pinch of salt and pepper
> ½ cup flour (approximately)
> Lemon wedges
> ¼ cup Caper Aioli (see page 18) or ¼ cup Marinara Sauce (see page 26), or both

1. Clean the squid, if not already cleaned (see Note). Cut the mantles into ½-inch-wide rings; leave the tentacle clusters whole. Rinse well and drain thoroughly.

2. Fill an electric deep fryer, a deep saucepan, or a Chinese wok with oil to a depth of at least 2 inches, leaving at least 2 inches vertical clearance from the top of the oil to the rim of the pan. Heat the oil to 350°F and turn the heat to low to just maintain the temperature.

3. Toss the cleaned and drained squid in a bowl with the Worcestershire sauce, salt, and pepper. Dredge the pieces in flour to coat them thoroughly, place them in a coarse strainer or frying basket, and shake off all the excess flour. Fry just until the coating is lightly browned and no longer tastes of raw flour, 45 to 60 seconds. Drain and serve immediately, with lemon wedges and your choice of sauces in small ramekins.

Notes: Control of the oil temperature is critical to good frying. A thermostatically controlled pan such as a deep fryer or electric wok is ideal; otherwise, use a clip-on frying thermometer. After frying, let the oil cool and strain it through several layers of cheesecloth into a clean, dry container. Seal tightly and it is good for two or three more rounds of frying.

It's possible to buy squid already cleaned, but it's cheaper if you clean it yourself. Start by separating all the tentacles from the heads, cutting across as close as possible to the eyes. Squeeze out and discard the hard, pea-sized beak in the center of each cluster of tentacles. Give the tentacles a quick rinse and drain them in a colander. To clean each mantle, grasp the mantle in one hand and the head in the other and pull apart; the entrails will pull out attached to the head. Pull the transparent quill out of the mantle. Discard everything but the tentacles and mantles. Running a little water into each mantle to open it up, reach in with a finger and pull out any entrails remaining inside. (Working over a second colander to catch all the debris will make cleanup easier.) There is no need to remove the spotted outer skin.

CHEESE-FLAVORED BREADSTICKS
── GRISSINI ──

A crunchy crust, the flavor of good cheese, and the take-another-they're-small size make these breadsticks irresistible. If you have a large crowd, the recipe can easily be doubled.

Makes about 3 dozen

> 2 to 2½ cups bread flour or all-purpose flour
> 1½ teaspoons fresh yeast (see Note, page 25)
> ¾ teaspoon granulated salt (double if using kosher salt)
> 2 tablespoons (approximately) olive oil
> ¼ cup plus 2 tablespoons grated Parmesan cheese
> ¾ cup plus 1 tablespoon tepid water

1. Place 2 cups of the flour in a large mixing bowl and crumble in the yeast. Stir in the salt, 1 tablespoon oil, and ¼ cup of the cheese. Add the water gradually and mix (with a wooden spoon, or with the dough hook if using a mixer) until the dough comes together; stop once or twice to scrape down the sides of the bowl. Knead, adding more flour as necessary, until the dough is very elastic and only slightly sticky (this can take 20 to 25 minutes even with a power mixer). Stretch and press the dough into a rectangle about 16 inches long, fold in the corners, and roll the dough into an even 16-inch cylinder. Lay the dough on a lightly floured sheet pan, brush the top with a little oil, cover, and let it rise until more than doubled in bulk, 1 to 2 hours.

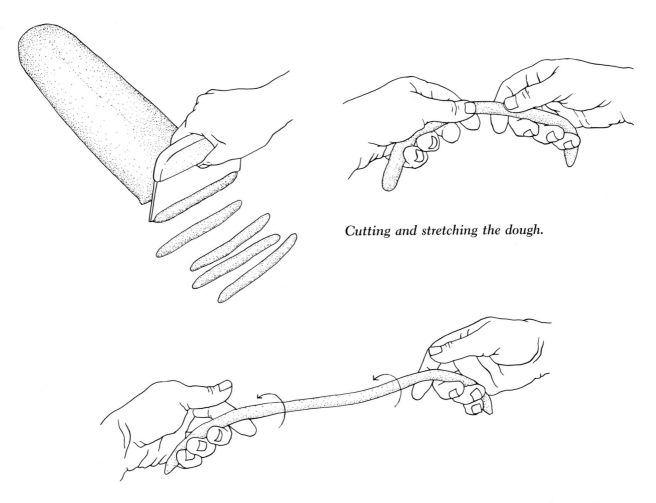

Cutting and stretching the dough.

2. Brush the risen loaf with a little more oil and dust the top lightly with grated cheese. Line 2 sheet pans with baking parchment. Using a bench scraper with a square-cornered metal blade, slice down through the loaf every ¼ inch or so, drawing the corner of the blade through against the pan to cut cleanly. Holding a strip of dough with both hands nearly meeting in the center, gently stretch the dough to about pencil thickness. Work your fingers out toward the ends as you swing and stretch the dough to about 14 inches long; roll the ends between your fingertips to thin them out to match the rest of the dough. Lay the sticks crosswise on the pans (they will shrink back to fit), about ¼ inch apart.

3. Preheat the oven to 375°F. Let the breadsticks rise until you can feel that they have puffed up slightly, about 15 minutes. Bake until golden brown outside but still white inside, 8 to 10 minutes. Serve as soon as they cool, or store in an airtight container for a day or two.

Note: This technique makes very crisp breadsticks. If you prefer them softer, give them a shorter rise after stretching and bake at 400°.

The trickiest thing about making breadsticks is getting them consistent in size, especially diameter. Even a slight difference in thickness means some parts will come out browned all the way through while others are still nearly white. Try to make the cuts of the original loaf as even as possible, and don't worry too much about length as long as the sticks come out the same diameter. If you stretch a section too thin, either press it back together a bit on the sheet pan or fold the stick in half and stretch it out again.

GRILLED GARLIC BREAD WITH TOMATOES

Bruschetta, the original garlic bread, is made with olive oil rather than the thick butter and cheese toppings so common in the United States. At its most basic, bruschetta is nothing more than grilled bread rubbed with raw garlic and brushed with oil, to be eaten out of hand. This version, though a little more fancy, is just as popular.

When the ingredients are as few and as basic as these, they must be of top quality. Use summer-ripe tomatoes, a good fruity olive oil, and a country-style bread with character. Newer Italian- and French-inspired bakeries in many cities now offer an array of delicious breads, including some with herbs, potato, or walnuts.

Serves 4

 7 tablespoons extra virgin olive oil
 2 small cloves garlic, mashed or
  pressed
1½ tablespoons balsamic vinegar
 1 teaspoon minced shallots
  Salt and freshly ground pepper, to
  taste

2 medium or 3 small tomatoes (about
 ¾ pound), seeded and coarsely
 diced
4 thick slices good crusty bread
2 cups arugula leaves, washed and
 dried

1. Combine 4 tablespoons of the oil with the garlic in a small bowl; set aside. Combine the remaining oil in a mixing bowl with the vinegar, shallots, salt, and pepper and stir to blend. Add the tomatoes and toss to coat.

2. Brush the bread slices on both sides with the garlic-flavored oil, brushing a bit of the garlic on at the same time. Grill over a moderate charcoal fire or broil until well toasted on both sides. Arrange the bread on a platter or individual plates. Lift the tomatoes out of the dressing and spread them on top of the toasts. Toss the arugula in the dressing remaining in the bowl and arrange it around the toasts.

GRILLED STUFFED FIGS
OR APRICOTS

In a twist on the traditional cold appetizer of figs and prosciutto, I like to stuff fresh figs with Gorgonzola, wrap them in pancetta, and grill them. Then I set them off with a little arugula salad for an unbeatable combination of sweet, salty, tart, and bitter flavors. This recipe is a great addition to a late-summer menu centered around the grill; earlier in the summer you can do the same thing with large apricots (see photo).

Serves 4

CHAMPAGNE VINAIGRETTE
1 tablespoon champagne vinegar
3 tablespoons extra virgin olive oil
  Scant teaspoon finely minced shallots
  Salt and freshly ground pepper, to taste

8 large figs or apricots, ripe but firm
2 ounces Gorgonzola cheese, rind removed
8 slices pancetta
2 cups arugula

1. To make the Champagne Vinaigrette, whisk together the vinegar, olive oil, and shallots. Add salt and pepper to taste, bearing in mind the saltiness of the pancetta. Set aside.

2. Remove the stems and partially split the figs lengthwise. (If using apricots, partially split them and remove the pits.) Gently spread apart the halves and stuff each fig with a scant tablespoon of cheese. Wrap each fig carefully in pancetta, enclosing the opening as thoroughly as possible. Skewer 2 or 3 figs together on thin skewers.

3. Grill the figs over a medium-hot fire until the pancetta is well browned all over (it helps to pull them off the skewers when nearly done to brown the unexposed parts). Some cheese will inevitably melt out into the fire. While the figs are grilling, toss the arugula in the vinaigrette (whisk the vinaigrette first it if has separated) and arrange a small heap in the center of a serving dish or individual plates. Arrange the grilled figs around the outside.

SOUPS, PASTAS, AND RISOTTOS

— ZUPPE, PASTE, E RISOTTI —

Potato and Leek Soup with Pancetta

Tomato, Sausage, and Focaccia Soup

White Bean and Polenta Soup

Vegetable and Bean Soup with Tortellini

About Pasta

Fresh Egg Noodle Dough

Tortellini in Gorgonzola Cream Sauce

Smoked Salmon Ravioli with Asparagus

Herbed Pappardelle with Chicken and Mushrooms

Pappardelle with Asparagus and Morels

Angel Hair Pasta with Tomatoes, Garlic, and Basil

Linguine with Clams

Angel Hair Pasta with Mussels and Pesto Cream

Pasta with Scallops in Spicy Tomato Sauce

Penne with Sun-Dried Tomatoes and Toasted Bread Crumbs

Penne with Lamb Sausage, Chard, and Ricotta

About Risotto

Basic Risotto Technique

Saffron Risotto with Scallops and Shrimp

Risotto with Smoked Chicken and Dried Cherries

Wild Mushroom Risotto

Risotto with Spring Vegetables

This may seem like an odd grouping of dishes for a chapter, but it reflects their role in a traditional Italian meal. Dishes that precede the main dish are known as *primi piatti,* or first courses. (Antipasto, even when it is a fairly substantial dish, doesn't qualify as a "course" in this scheme of things.) Depending on the time of day and the rest of the menu, the *primo* may be a soup, a pasta dish, or the uniquely Italian style of cooked rice known as risotto. In general, when one of this trio is served in a meal, the others are not.

These days, when lighter meals are the rule both here and in Italy, *primi* sometimes become the main dish. Along with some good bread and a salad, a hearty soup, pasta, or risotto can be plenty for lunch or supper.

Soups are more typical of the evening *cena* (supper) than the larger midday dinner or *pranzo.* Italian soups tend to be earthy and hearty rather than refined and delicate, and they often include beans or bread to give them extra substance. A few of our best sellers are included here.

Pasta is as firmly established in American cooking as it is in Italian, and for good reason. It's inexpensive, convenient, and versatile; it combines well with all sorts of vegetables, meats, seafood, cheeses, and herbs for a nearly infinite variety of dishes. Whether you serve it as a first course in the Italian style or as a main dish, pasta is one of the most satisfying foods of the Mediterranean diet. We use both fresh (homemade) and dried (factory-made) pasta in the restaurant, and recipes using both appear in this chapter.

Like pasta, risotto—short-grain Italian Arborio rice braised in broth—can be a carrier for all sorts of savory flavors. And like pasta, it is usually a first course in Italy. There are occasional exceptions, as in the eggplant risotto that accompanies the lamb chops on page 132, but otherwise it's strictly a *primo.* Still, a risotto dressed up with seafood, mushrooms, meats, or poultry, especially when enriched with butter or cheese, can easily function as a main dish in a lighter meal.

POTATO AND LEEK SOUP
WITH PANCETTA

This soup could be pureed in the manner of a French leek soup, but I prefer the more rustic character that comes from random-sized chunks of potatoes.

Serves 6 to 8

> 1 pound leeks
> 3 ounces pancetta, sliced ⅛ inch thick and diced
> 2 tablespoons butter
> ½ cup diced onion
> 3 medium russet potatoes (about 1¼ pounds), peeled and cut into 1-inch cubes
> 3 cups Chicken Stock (see page 34)
> 1 bay leaf
> ½ cup cream
> 1 teaspoon salt
> ¼ teaspoon grated nutmeg
> ½ teaspoon white pepper
> ¼ cup grated Parmesan cheese

1. Rinse the leeks and remove the root ends and any damaged outer leaves. Split each leek lengthwise. Starting at the base, cut the halves into ¼-inch diagonal slices; stop when the tops are becoming more green than yellow. Put the slices into a deep bowl of water and work them up and down with your hands to dislodge any dirt. Let the dirt settle, then lift the leeks out of the water and drain well.

2. Combine the pancetta and butter in a large, heavy-bottomed soup pan (see Note, page 63). Cook over medium heat until the pancetta is well browned. Add the diced onion and cook until lightly browned. Add the potatoes and leeks and cook, stirring frequently so the potatoes do not scorch, until the leeks are soft, about 10 minutes. Add the stock and bay leaf and simmer until the potatoes are tender, about 45 minutes. Add the cream, salt, nutmeg, and pepper. Taste for seasoning and adjust if necessary. Stir in the cheese.

TOMATO, SAUSAGE, AND FOCACCIA SOUP

Soups thickened with leftover bread are among the most basic and ancient of Italian foods. They go under various names—*pancotto, ribollita, pappa al pomodoro,* and many others. This version with sausage might be a luxury in the peasant-food tradition, but it's still an economical and nutritious way to make a little sausage go a long way. You can make it more or less spicy by your choice of sausage and the amount of red pepper flakes you use.

Serves 6

⅓ pound uncooked Italian-style sausage
1 cup finely diced onion
½ cup finely diced celery
½ small red bell pepper, seeded and finely diced
½ tablespoon minced garlic
2½ pounds ripe pear tomatoes, peeled, seeded, and cut into 8 pieces each
1 cup chicken stock
1 small bay leaf
1 teaspoon minced fresh tarragon
2 teaspoons minced fresh basil
Pinch of red pepper flakes
½ teaspoon fennel seed, ground
¾ teaspoon salt, or to taste
½ small lemon
2½ ounces leftover Focaccia (see page 22)
Extra virgin olive oil
Grated Parmesan cheese

1. Puncture the sausage casings well with a fork or the tip of a knife. Place the sausages in a large heavy-bottomed soup pan (see Note) and add about ¼ inch of water. Bring to a boil, reduce the heat to medium, and simmer until the water has evaporated and the sausage begins to brown in its rendered fat. Add the onion, celery, and bell pepper and cook, stirring often, until the vegetables are soft. Remove the sausages, add the garlic, and continue cooking until all the vegetables have absorbed the flavor of the sausage drippings (taste a bit to see).

2. Add the tomatoes to the pan and cook until they become soft and release a lot of juice. Add the stock, bay leaf, herbs, red pepper flakes, fennel seed, and salt. Squeeze the lemon through a strainer into the soup, discard the seeds, and add the squeezed lemon half to the pan. Simmer 10 minutes, or until the flavors are blended. Discard the lemon. Split the sausages lenthwise, cut them into bite-size pieces, and return them to the soup.

3. Cut the focaccia into 1-inch cubes and add it to the soup. Simmer until the soup is well thickened, stirring to break up the pieces of bread. Taste for seasoning and correct if necessary. Drizzle each serving with a little olive oil and top with a bit of grated cheese.

Notes: The soup can be prepared a day or more ahead of time through step 2 and refrigerated. Add the bread on serving day.

This soup and the next one start with a browning step, so it's important to use a pan with a heavy bottom and a large enough base to give plenty of browning surface. In the restaurant we use a relatively shallow, straight-sided pan called a *rondeau;* at home a flameproof casserole or a good-sized saucepan will do.

WHITE BEAN
AND POLENTA SOUP

I don't know if there is any Italian precedent for combining beans and polenta in a soup. Frankly, I got the idea from a dish served at another San Francisco restaurant, the Zuni Cafe. Traditional or not, it's a flavorful, stick-to-the-ribs soup for a chilly evening.

Serves 10

>   2 cups small dry white beans
>   1 ham hock (about 1 pound)
>   8 cups Chicken Stock (see page 34)
>   2 bay leaves
>   2 teaspoons salt
>   ½ cup coarse corn meal (polenta)
>   2 tablespoons butter
>   1½ cups finely diced onion
>   1 cup finely diced celery
>   ½ cup finely diced carrot
>   ½ cup finely diced red bell pepper

1. Pick over the beans well, discarding any broken, shriveled, or discolored beans or pebbles. Combine the beans in a large pot with the ham hock, stock, bay leaves, and salt. Bring to a boil, reduce the heat, and simmer uncovered until the beans are tender, 2 to 2½ hours. Keep an eye on the liquid level as the beans cook, and add additional stock or water if necessary to keep it from dropping below the level of the beans.

2. When the beans are tender, remove the ham hock and set it aside to cool; discard the bay leaves. Stir the polenta into the soup and keep it at a simmer, stirring occasionally. Meanwhile, melt the butter in a skillet over medium heat and add the diced vegetables. Saute until the onions are soft and everything is lightly browned and well flavored. Add the contents of the skillet to the soup pot. Skin the ham hock and pull the meat off the bones. Dice the meat, discarding any gristly parts. Add the diced meat to the soup, taste for seasoning, and serve.

Note: The soup can be made entirely ahead of time and reheated.

Vegetable and Bean Soup with Tortellini (page 69)

VEGETABLE AND BEAN SOUP WITH TORTELLINI

Soups combining pasta and beans (*pasta e fagioli*) are popular throughout Italy. If you start the whole thing from scratch, this can be a time-consuming dish to make, but if you keep some cooked beans on hand and have some leftover ravioli or tortellini in the freezer, you can put it together in a few minutes. Vary the vegetables according to what is in season: corn, zucchini, yellow squash, or green beans in summer; hard squashes in fall; cabbage, cauliflower, or broccoli in winter; asparagus or peas in spring.

Serves 4

- ½ recipe Tomato Pasta Dough (see Variation, page 72)
- ½ recipe Ricotta filling (see Tortellini in Gorgonzola Cream Sauce, page 74)
- 2 tablespoons olive oil
- 2 cloves garlic, sliced
- 3 green onions, sliced ¼ inch long
- ½ cup assorted seasonal vegetables, finely diced (see introduction)
- 3 medium mushrooms, sliced
- ½ cup cooked small white beans
- 3 ounces smoked ham, shredded by hand (about ¼ cup)
- 2 cups chicken or veal stock (see page 34)
- ½ cup seeded and diced tomato
  Salt and freshly ground pepper to taste

Chopped chives or thinly sliced basil leaves, for garnish
Shaved Parmesan cheese, for garnish (optional)

1. Prepare the tomato pasta dough through the first step. While the dough rests, combine the filling ingredients in a bowl and mix thoroughly. Knead and roll out the dough as described on page 71, rolling it out to the second-thinnest setting on the pasta machine. Use the dough and filling to make tortellini as directed on page 74, or ravioli as directed on page 77.

2. Boil the tortellini in a large pot of salted water until tender, 4 to 5 minutes. Meanwhile, heat the oil in a large skillet over medium-high heat. Add the garlic, green onions, diced vegetables, and mushrooms and cook until the onion wilts. Add the beans, ham, stock, and tomato and cook until the beans are heated through. Season to taste (if the ham is especially salty, no additional salt may be needed).

3. Drain the cooked tortellini and place them in large shallow soup bowls. Ladle the broth and vegetables over the top. Garnish with chives or basil and shavings of Parmesan if desired. Serve immediately.

ABOUT PASTA

Some recipes in this book call for fresh pasta, some for dried. There is a widespread misconception in this country that fresh pasta is inherently better than dried. Not only is this untrue, they are two entirely different and rarely interchangeable categories of food.

Dried pasta consists of nothing but hard durum wheat flour (semolina) and water, made into a paste (the literal meaning of pasta), formed into various shapes, and dried. In the United States, it's often labeled "macaroni product" to distinguish it from "noodles," which by American law must contain egg. We use only imported Italian pasta, which has a firmer feel when cooked than most domestic pasta; DiCecco and Delverde are two good brands.

Just as fresh and dried pasta are not interchangeable, each shape of dried pasta has its own qualities. Some are smoother and more slippery, others have holes and grooves which trap bits of sauce; each recipe calls for the shape which we think is most appropriate. *Linguine*, long and narrow noodles with a slightly oval cross section, are traditional with seafood, but ordinary spaghetti will do as a substitute. For tomato sauces and sauces with a lot of olive oil, we like to use shorter cuts such as *penne*, short ridged or smooth tubes with diagonally cut ends; similar cuts are labeled *mostaccioli* or *pennoni*, and other short tube shapes such as *rigatoni* are also suitable. We also use shells, *orecchiete*, and other small cuts in garnishes for entrees, such as the Osso Buco on page 130.

Fresh pasta is made from flour and eggs, sometimes with a little oil and water added to the dough, and is both shaped and cooked while still soft and pliable. We use it when we want a more tender and absorbent noodle, especially with sauces based on stock or cream. The *pappardelle* on page 78 is a perfect example; the extra-wide noodles are designed to drink up the rich reduced-broth sauce. Of course, fresh pasta is essential for making ravioli, tortellini, and other stuffed pasta shapes. A home pasta machine makes easy work of rolling and stretching the dough to sheets of the ideal thickness, which can then be cut into the appropriate shape of noodle or pieces for stuffing.

The one cut of pasta used in this book for which macaroni and egg pasta can be considered interchangeable is angel hair (*capellini* or *capelli d'angelo*). These very fine strands are available in both forms, and they cook to nearly identical results, so use whichever is readily available.

FRESH
EGG NOODLE DOUGH

Fresh, homemade pasta is not necessarily better than factory-made dried pasta; it's just different. Both have a place in good Italian cooking. Fresh pasta cooks more quickly, has a slightly more tender feel in the mouth, and absorbs sauces better than dried pasta. It's also more variable; you can cut it into any width or shape you like, and flavor it with herbs, spinach, tomato, or other flavorings to suit the dish. And, of course, fresh pasta is essential for making ravioli, tortellini, and other stuffed pasta shapes. For all these reasons, fresh pasta should be part of every cook's repertoire.

My pasta recipe uses a higher proportion of semolina to all-purpose flour than is typical of many fresh pastas. It makes a firm but pliable dough that is easy to handle, and has an *al dente* "bite" more like that of dry pasta. If you prefer a more tender noodle, especially for ravioli and other stuffed shapes, feel free to substitute more all-purpose flour for some of the semolina.

The recipes here are designed for a home pasta machine, the kind with rollers that adjust from about 3/32 inch to less than 1/64 inch apart. (Because of the elasticity of the dough, the distance between the rollers does not exactly match the thickness of the pasta, which generally comes out a little thicker.)

Makes 1 pound

    1 cup semolina flour
    1 cup all-purpose flour, plus more for
        dusting
    2 large eggs
    2 teaspoons salt
    2 teaspoons olive oil
    3 tablespoons water, or more as needed

1. *To make the dough in an electric mixer,* combine all the ingredients except the water in the mixer bowl and mix with a dough hook just until the dough comes together; add water as needed to moisten the dough to a smooth, slightly sticky consistency. Remove the ball, wrap it in plastic, and let it rest at least 15 minutes before rolling. *To make in a food processor,* combine all the ingredients including the water and process with a pulsing action until the dough forms small, moist pellets about the size of couscous grains that stick together when squeezed; add a little more water if the mixture is too dry. Press the dough together into a flat cake, wrap it in plastic, and let it rest at least 15 minutes before rolling. *To mix by hand,* combine the semolina and all-purpose flour and form them into a mound on a work surface. Make a well in the center and put the remaining ingredients in the well. Mix the wet ingredients together with a fork, gradually incorporating the flours. Mix with the fork until the mixture becomes too heavy and sticky, then switch to kneading by hand, using a square-edged pastry scraper to gather up bits of dough sticking to the board. Continue kneading until the dough is smooth and no longer sticky, adding a little more flour if necessary. There is no need to let hand-mixed dough rest at this point.

2. Divide the dough into two or three pieces, for easier handling. Knead each piece by hand briefly, adding all-purpose flour as needed to keep it from sticking to the board. Flatten one piece of dough slightly with the heel of your hand and put it through the thickest setting on your pasta machine (keep the rest of the dough covered to prevent drying). Don't worry if the dough comes out of the machine in many pieces; just put them

together slightly overlapped and put the whole piece through again. When the whole piece goes through without tearing, fold it in half, dust the outside liberally with flour, and roll it out again. Continue doubling, dusting, and re-rolling the dough until it rolls out easily and smoothly, six to 10 times through in all. Set the pasta machine for the next thinnest setting and put the sheet through again (do not fold it in half anymore). Continue to dust well with flour before and after rolling. Continue reducing the thickness to the desired setting, usually the last or next to last setting available on the machine.

3. Dust the finished sheets of pasta with flour or semolina and set them aside until you are ready to cut them into noodles or make them into tortellini, ravioli, or other stuffed shapes. If the dough has the right consistency, the sheets can sit for up to a half hour before cutting, but don't let them dry out to the point that they are brittle.

Technique Note: Getting the proper feel for pasta dough takes some practice. When you first mix the dough, it should be dry enough that it does not stick to the bowl or the table, but moist enough that you can gather it together into a cohesive ball. In the rolling-out stage, dough that is too dry will crumble rather than stretch. You can easily add more flour in the rolling stage if the dough is a bit sticky, but adding water to a dry, crumbly dough is more difficult. In general, a slightly drier dough is best for noodles, a slightly softer, tackier texture for stuffed pasta shapes.

Variation: *Spinach Pasta Dough*
I used to think that spinach had to be blanched, drained, and squeezed to rid it of its moisture before being made into pasta dough. I learned differently one day at Kuleto's as I watched prep cook Fidel Perez throw raw spinach into a blender with the eggs. It worked fine, and this is how I have made spinach pasta ever since:

Add 2 generous cups of washed and drained spinach leaves (about 1½ ounces after removing the stems) to the basic recipe above. Omit the water, as the spinach provides plenty. If making the dough in a food processor, add the leaves whole at the beginning of the process; they will be chopped sufficiently as the machine processes the dough. If using a mixer or making the pasta by hand, chop the leaves as finely as possible with a knife and add them along with the egg. The added spinach will make a slightly larger volume of dough than the basic recipe.

Variation: *Tomato Pasta Dough*
Add 4 tablespoons tomato paste to the basic pasta dough recipe along with the eggs. Use this dough for ravioli or other stuffed pasta shapes (to be served with sauces other than tomato).

Variation: *Herb Pasta Dough*
Add a chopped fresh herb (dill, oregano, and rosemary are good choices) along with the eggs. Be sure the herb is compatible with the dish in which it will be used, and does not duplicate or compete with another herb in the sauce. Dill pasta, for example, is ideal with salmon, as in the Smoked Salmon Ravioli on page 77. For Herbed Papardelle with Chicken and Mushrooms (page 78), we use a blend of fresh herbs including basil, oregano, parsley, tarragon, sage, and thyme. The amount of herb to use depends on its natural intensity of flavor; with a delicate herb like dill you'll need as much as 1 cup for its flavor to come through, but with rosemary as little as 2 tablespoons will do.

Variation: *Saffron Pasta Dough*
Crumble 1 teaspoon saffron threads into a small bowl and add 3 tablespoons boiling water. Let steep 10 minutes or more, then use the water (with the saffron) in place of the water in the basic recipe. I like saffron pasta mainly with seafood, with either cream or a lightly cooked tomato sauce. It's suitable for either noodles or stuffed shapes.

Tortellini in Gorgonzola Cream Sauce (page 74)

73

TORTELLINI IN GORGONZOLA CREAM SAUCE

Some might argue that these stuffed pasta bundles are too large to be called *tortellini*. It's true that most tortellini are smaller than these; but having tried it both ways, I find that the flavor of the filling comes through better in this larger two-bite size than it does in the traditional bite-size dumplings. And making them larger cuts down on preparation time, since you only have to make about half as many. Even so, allow yourself plenty of time for rolling out the dough and stuffing and folding the tortellini; better yet, get a friend or family member to pitch in.

Serves 4

1 recipe Fresh Egg Noodle Dough
(page 71)

RICOTTA FILLING
½ pound whole milk ricotta cheese
1 tablespoon minced shallots
½ tablespoon minced garlic
2 tablespoons thinly sliced and diced
    prosciutto

1 tablespoon chopped mixed fresh
    herbs (parsley, tarragon, basil)
1 tablespoon dry seasoned bread
    crumbs
½ teaspoon salt
⅛ teaspoon freshly ground pepper

GORGONZOLA CREAM SAUCE
2 tablespoons minced shallots
2 cups chopped radicchio (½ large
    head)
2 tablespoons olive oil
1 cup cream
6 ounces Gorgonzola cheese, diced
2 tablespoons grated Parmesan cheese
    Freshly ground black pepper, to
    taste

1. Prepare the noodle dough up to the point of wrapping and resting. While the dough rests, combine the filling ingredients in a bowl and mix thoroughly.

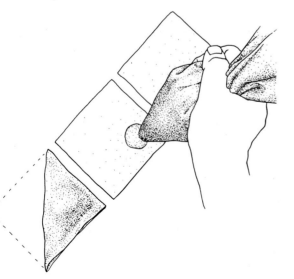

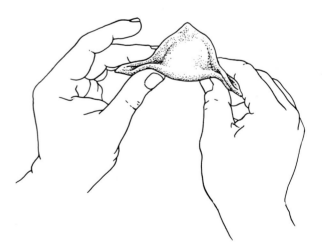

2. Knead and roll out the dough as described on page 71, rolling it out to the second-thinnest setting on the pasta machine. Dust a finished sheet of dough liberally with semolina, then fold one end over to meet the other end and trim the ends square. Fold the doubled sheet in half or thirds again, to create a rectangle just over 6 inches long. Trim all sides with a sharp knife to make a 3 × 6-inch rectangle, then cut it in half to make two stacks of 3-inch squares. Repeat with the remaining sheet(s) of dough as needed to make about 32 squares in all; reserve the trimmings to cut into fettucine or other noodles.

3. Lay out a few squares of dough on the table; keep the rest covered with plastic wrap or a towel. With a pastry bag or spoon, place about 1½ teaspoons of filling near one corner of each square. Moisten the opposite edges of the dough with a little water and fold over, making a neat triangle. Press the edges together to seal. Holding the triangle with the square corner away from you, pinch the other two corners about an inch in from the tips so the edges are doubled (see illustration). Place one finger under the center and draw the two points together underneath it,

pinching them together well to seal. Repeat with the remaining pasta and filling.

4. Cook the tortellini in boiling water until the thickest part of the pasta is done, about 5 minutes. While the pasta cooks, make the sauce in a large skillet: Saute the shallots and radicchio in the oil until the radicchio is wilted. Add the cream and simmer until slightly reduced. Stir in the cheeses and season to taste with pepper. Drain the cooked tortellini, toss them in the sauce, and serve immediately.

Variation: For green tortellini, use Spinach Pasta Dough (see Variation, page 72). At the restaurant we make both green and white, *verdi e bianchi*, and serve a few of each on each plate.

Technique Note: If you are very careful in rolling out the dough and make sure it goes the full width of the rollers, it is possible to get two rows of squares from a sheet of pasta. However, after trimming they will probably come out no bigger than 2½ inches square, and the difference in size is more than you might think ½ inch would make. I would rather cut a single row of squares a full 3 inches square and cut the trimmings into noodles.

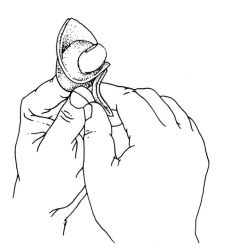

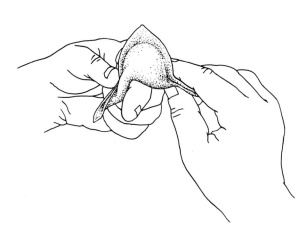

SMOKED SALMON RAVIOLI WITH ASPARAGUS

Smoked salmon is a recent addition to northern Italian cooking, but it has become firmly established in dishes such as this. A strong lemon flavor from both juice and zest helps balance the richness of the sauce as well as preventing the salmon flavor from becoming the least bit fishy.

Serves 2 to 3

- ½ recipe Herb Pasta, made with ½ cup fresh dill (see Variation, page 72)
- 3 ounces cold-smoked salmon, thinly sliced
- 2 tablespoons mascarpone (or cream cheese thinned with a tiny amount of milk)
- 1 tablespoon olive oil
- 2 teaspoons minced shallots
- ½ cup dry white wine
- ¾ cup cream
- 5 or 6 medium asparagus spears, sliced diagonally (to make ½ cup)
- Juice and grated zest of ½ small lemon
- Salt, to taste

1. Cut out 24 2-inch squares of pasta; reserve the rest for another use. Cut the smoked salmon into 24 equal pieces, each about 1 inch square. Center a piece of salmon on half of the pasta squares, top each with about ½ teaspoon of mascarpone, then add another piece of salmon. Brush the edges of the pasta squares with a tiny bit of water, top with the remaining pasta squares, and press to seal the edges well, forcing out any pockets of air. Set the ravioli aside on a sheet pan dusted with flour or semolina; cover with a towel to keep them from drying out.

2. Have a pot of lightly salted boiling water ready to cook the ravioli. Heat the oil in a skillet over medium heat and cook the shallots just until soft; do not brown. Add the wine, reduce slightly, and add the cream, asparagus, lemon juice and zest, and a pinch of salt. Cook the ravioli while the sauce reduces slightly. When the ravioli are done, in about 3 minutes, drain and toss them in the sauce to coat them. Lift the ravioli out of the sauce with a slotted spoon or tongs and arrange them on warmed plates with the asparagus on top; pour the sauce over all.

Technique Note: This one-at-a-time method is only one of the possible ways of making ravioli. If you have a ravioli plate, a ravioli attachment on a pasta machine, or any other favorite method, by all means use it.

Herbed Pappardelle with Chicken and Mushrooms

Although this is one of the simplest pasta dishes we make at Kuleto's (or maybe because of its simplicity), it has always been one of my favorites. Together with a salad it makes a satisfying lunch or light supper, though you could serve it in smaller portions as a first course before a fish entree. This version uses ordinary commercial mushrooms. Of course, if you use other varieties of mushrooms, such as porcini, chanterelles, hedgehog, or oyster mushrooms, the flavor will be that much better.

Serves 2

        2 tablespoons olive oil
        6 ounces boneless chicken breast, cut
            in large dice
    1½ cups thickly sliced mushrooms
        1 teaspoon minced garlic
        2 teaspoons minced shallots
        4 to 5 ounces fresh Herb Pasta Dough
            (see Variation, page 72) cut into
            1-inch-wide noodles (*pappardelle*)
        1 cup chicken or veal stock (see Note,
            page 34)
        2 tablespoons sliced green onions
        2 teaspoons chopped tarragon leaves
            Salt and freshly ground pepper, to
            taste
        2 tablespoons butter
        1 tablespoon toasted pine nuts

1. Have a pot of lightly salted boiling water ready to cook the noodles. Heat the oil in a skillet and saute the chicken until nearly opaque. Add the mushrooms, garlic, and shallots and cook until the mushrooms begin to brown. Meanwhile, separate the noodles and drop them into the boiling water.

2. Add the stock, green onions, and tarragon to the skillet and cook over high heat until reduced slightly. Season to taste and swirl in the butter. Remove the skillet from the heat if the noodles are not yet ready.

3. Drain the cooked noodles and toss them in the skillet to coat them with the sauce, carefully separating the noodles so they get evenly moistened. Serve the noodles on heated plates or in shallow bowls, arranging the chicken and mushrooms on top; garnish with pine nuts.

PAPPARDELLE WITH ASPARAGUS AND MORELS

Here's another variation on the theme of pappardelle with mushrooms, specifically for the month of May when both asparagus and wild morels are in season.

Serves 2

 4 to 6 ounces fresh morels
 ¼ pound fresh asparagus
 2 tablespoons olive oil
 1 teaspoon minced shallots
 1 cup Brown Veal Stock (page 34; see Note)
 3 tablespoons dry Madeira
 ½ pound Fresh Egg Noodle Dough (page 71), cut into 1-inch-wide noodles (*pappardelle*)
 1 teaspoon fresh tarragon leaves
 Salt and freshly ground pepper, to taste

1. Split the morels lengthwise and brush away any visible dirt. Snap off the tough bases of the asparagus and slice the stalks diagonally into 1-inch pieces. Have ready a pot of salted water for boiling the noodles.

2. Heat the oil in a skillet over high heat and add the shallots, morels, and asparagus. Saute until the mushrooms begin to soften, about 2 minutes. Add the stock and wine and reduce by half. Meanwhile, cook the noodles. Add the tarragon to the sauce and season to taste. Drain the cooked noodles and toss them in the skillet to coat them with sauce. Serve immediately, arranging the asparagus and mushrooms on top.

Note: A rich stock is essential in both this and the preceding recipe, as it provides most of the body in the sauce. The Brown Veal Stock on page 34 is ideal, but a good homemade chicken stock reduced by half will do.

ANGEL HAIR PASTA WITH TOMATOES, GARLIC, AND BASIL

Good ripe tomatoes, sweet basil, fine olive oil, and a hefty dose of garlic add up to the most popular pasta sauce at Kuleto's. If you can't get good ripe tomatoes, don't bother with this dish.

We offer grated Parmesan with this pasta at the table because so many of our customers expect it, but I don't think the sauce needs it and I don't add any myself.

Serves 4

- ¼ cup thinly sliced garlic
- 7 tablespoons extra virgin olive oil
- 2 cups seeded and diced tomatoes (about 1 pound)
- ⅔ cup basil leaves, roughly chopped
- ¾ teaspoon kosher salt, or to taste
  Freshly ground black pepper, to taste
- 6 ounces dried angel hair pasta (*capellini* or *capelli d'angelo*)

Combine the garlic and 3 tablespoons of the oil in a skillet over medium heat. Cook slowly until the garlic is lightly and evenly browned. Reduce the heat to low, add the tomatoes, basil, salt, and pepper, and cook just until the tomatoes are heated through. Meanwhile, cook the pasta in ample salted boiling water. Drain the cooked pasta and add it and the remaining oil to the skillet. Toss to coat the pasta with the oil. Serve in warmed bowls, with the tomatoes and basil on top.

LINGUINE WITH CLAMS

Italian purists call me on this dish all the time. I know that in Italy *linguine alle vongole* would never have cream in it, let alone pancetta. But this dish is one of our most popular offerings, so who am I to argue with success?

Serves 4

½ cup chopped pancetta
1 tablespoon olive oil
24 small live clams, well scrubbed
2 teaspoons *each* minced garlic and shallots
6 ounces dried linguine or other long, thin dried pasta
¾ cup dry white wine
1 cup cream
2 tablespoons chopped fresh basil leaves
1 tablespoon chopped fresh tarragon
⅔ cup diced tomatoes
½ teaspoon salt
½ teaspoon freshly ground pepper, or to taste
1 to 2 tablespoons butter (optional)

Combine the pancetta, oil, clams, garlic, and shallots in a large skillet over high heat. Cook until the pancetta begins to render its fat and the clams begin to open. At this point, start cooking the pasta in rapidly boiling salted water. Add the wine, cream, herbs, tomatoes, salt, and pepper to the skillet and reduce slightly. Taste for seasoning and adjust if necessary. Add the butter if you want a richer flavor. When the pasta is done, drain it well, add it to the skillet, and toss to coat it evenly with sauce. Divide the pasta into warmed bowls and spoon the clams and sauce over the top. Discard any clams that have not opened by this point.

ANGEL HAIR PASTA WITH MUSSELS AND PESTO CREAM

This dish is as attractive as it is delicious. The pale green of the pesto-flavored cream sets off the blue-black mussel shells, the creamy-orange mussel meat, and the red tomatoes.

Serves 4

- 1 tablespoon olive oil
- 2 dozen small mussels, cleaned (see Note)
- 1 teaspoon minced garlic
- 2 teaspoons minced shallots
- ¾ cup dry white wine
- 1 teaspoon lemon juice
- ½ cup cream
- 2 tablespoons Pesto (page 29)
- 6 ounces dried angel hair pasta (*capellini* or *capelli d'angelo*)
- ½ cup cooked small white beans (see page 115)
- Salt and freshly ground pepper, to taste
- ½ cup finely diced unpeeled tomatoes

1. Combine the oil, mussels, garlic, and shallots in a large skillet over high heat. Cook until the mussels begin to open. Add the wine, lemon juice, cream, and pesto and reduce slightly. Meanwhile, start cooking the pasta in rapidly boiling salted water.

2. When the mussel shells are all open, add the beans to the sauce and season to taste. Arrange the mussels around the outside of a serving dish or individual pasta bowls and spoon a little sauce into each shell. Drain the cooked pasta and add it to the skillet, toss to coat it with sauce, and arrange it in the middle of the dish or bowls. Garnish the ring of mussels with diced tomato and serve immediately.

Note: To clean mussels, grasp the "beard" (the bundle of fibers coming out one side of the shell) and pull it off with a quick tug. Rinse well, and if the shells are at all dirty, scrub them with a brush. Discard any open mussels that show no sign of closing when handled (the response can be slow in cold mussels, but they should move perceptibly).

PASTA WITH SCALLOPS IN SPICY TOMATO SAUCE

This dish relies on top-quality scallops. I am fussy about the scallops I buy for the restaurant. I pay a premium for fresh "day boat" scallops, meaning the boats come in with their catch each day rather than fishing for several days at a time. When buying fresh scallops, look for those that are on the dry side rather than sitting in a pool of liquid; those in liquid may have been soaked in water to increase their weight. Good fresh scallops may even be dry to the point of being a bit sticky, which is fine as long as they have no strong or fishy odors.

Serves 4

>   ½ pound angel hair, vermicelli, spaghettini, or other thin pasta
> 12 ounces medium scallops
>   Flour for dusting
>   3 tablespoons olive oil
>   1 tablespoon minced shallots
>   1 teaspoon red pepper flakes, or to taste
> 1½ ounces Pernod
> 2½ cups Marinara Sauce I (see page 26)
>   3 tablespoons extra virgin olive oil
> 12 large basil leaves

1. Have ready a pot of salted boiling water for cooking the pasta. When to add the pasta will depend on the cut; time it to be done at the same time as the sauce.

2. Dust the scallops in flour, shaking off the excess. Heat the olive oil in a large skillet over medium-high heat. Add the scallops and brown them nicely on both sides, about 2 minutes per side. Remove them to a warm plate and set aside.

3. Add the shallots and pepper flakes to the skillet and cook until fragrant. Add the Pernod, bring to a boil, and touch a long lighted match to the pan to burn off the alcohol. Add the marinara sauce, bring to a boil, and cook until the flavors blend. Correct the seasoning if necessary.

4. Spoon the sauce into 4 large flat plates. Arrange the scallops in a ring around the edge of each plate. Drain the cooked pasta and toss it with the extra virgin oil. For each serving twist a quarter of the pasta in a coil around a fork and arrange it in the center of the plate. To garnish, roll the basil leaves together and slice them into fine ribbons (chiffonade).

Variation: Other shellfish can be substituted for the scallops. Saute medium to large raw shrimp whole. The very largest sizes can be cut crosswise into medallions, as can lobster tail meat.

Note: Pernod is really the only anise liqueur I recommend for this dish. Sambuca may be more Italian, but it's way too sweet, and it upsets the balance of the dish. If you don't have any Pernod, add ½ teaspoon of crushed anise seeds to the pan along with the pepper flakes.

PENNE
WITH SUN-DRIED TOMATOES
AND TOASTED
BREAD CRUMBS

Northern Italian influences dominate our menu, but we're happy to use southern techniques when the results are as delicious as this dish, in which olive oil and bread crumbs make up the "sauce." Try it with any vegetable of the broccoli family, including cauliflower, the beautiful pale green Romanesco broccoli, or the thinner, stronger-tasting relative variously known as *broccoli raab, broccoli rabe,* or *rapini.*

Serves 2 to 4

> 6 ounces penne, mostaccioli, or other short tubular dried pasta
> ¼ cup olive oil
> ¼ cup fine bread crumbs
> 2 teaspoons minced garlic
> ½ cup broccoli or cauliflower florets, blanched or steamed
> ¼ cup reconstituted sun-dried tomatoes, chopped (see page 35)
> 1 teaspoon minced fresh rosemary
> Salt and freshly ground pepper, to taste
> 3 tablespoons extra virgin olive oil
> 2½ ounces fresh mozzarella, in ½-inch cubes (room temperature)

1. Start the pasta cooking in ample boiling salted water. Heat the oil in a large skillet over medium heat. Sprinkle in the bread crumbs and cook, stirring, until the crumbs are golden brown. Add the garlic and cook a few seconds, or until fragrant. Add the broccoli, tomatoes, and rosemary and cook until heated through. Season to taste. Remove from the heat if ready before the pasta is done.

2. Drain the pasta quickly and add it to the skillet. Let a little of the cooking water cling to the pasta; it will become part of the sauce. Add the extra virgin oil and cheese and toss to combine. Serve immediately, on warm plates.

PENNE WITH LAMB SAUSAGE, CHARD, AND RICOTTA

This is one of our most popular pasta dishes; in fact, we make about 50 pounds of lamb sausage every week just for this dish. It's easy to see why it's popular. The smoothness of the ricotta rounds out the spicy flavors of the sausage, the slight astringency of the chard, and the sweet-tart tomato sauce.

Serves 4

- ½ pound Lamb Sausage (see page 33)
- 1 tablespoon olive oil
- ½ pound penne or mostaccioli
- 2 tablespoons minced shallots
- 2 teaspoons minced garlic
- 4 large leaves red chard, any tough parts of stems removed, chopped
- 1 cup Marinara Sauce I or II (page 26)
  Salt and freshly ground pepper, to taste
- ¼ cup ricotta cheese

1. If the sausage is in a casing, slit it open and remove the casing; if you are using bulk sausage, form it into two patties. Heat the oil over medium heat and brown the sausages on both sides, breaking them apart as they begin to brown. Meanwhile, start cooking the pasta in boiling salted water.

2. When the sausage has lost nearly all its raw color, add the shallots and garlic to the pan. Cook another minute or so, then add the chard and cook until wilted. Add the marinara sauce and cook until heated through. Taste for seasoning and correct if necessary.

3. Drain the cooked pasta and toss it in the sauce in the skillet or a warmed serving bowl. Serve into individual bowls with a dollop of ricotta on top of each serving.

Variation: This recipe also works fine with Italian-style sausages, either bought or homemade (see page 32). Puncture the sausage casings well with a fork or the tip of a knife. Place the sausages in a large heavy-bottomed skillet and add water to cover the bottom by about ¼ inch. Bring to a boil, reduce the heat to medium, and simmer until the water has evaporated and the sausages begin to brown in their rendered fat. Remove and slice the sausages, return them to the pan, start the pasta cooking, and proceed with step 2.

ABOUT RISOTTO

Risotto is a uniquely Italian method of cooking rice. Just about everywhere else in the world, the cooking liquid is added to the rice (or vice versa) all at once. What distinguishes risotto is the way the liquid, usually a meat or seafood broth, is added in stages and cooked to the point of absorption after each addition. And whereas stirring rice while it cooks is all wrong in most other methods, it is essential to making risotto.

The result of the risotto technique is a texture unlike that of any other rice dish. I love the way Chez Panisse chef Paul Bertolli describes risotto as "a marriage of rice and broth," and I always quote him when training a new cook to make this dish. In a good risotto, every grain of rice has its own identity at the center, but it is bound to the rest by a creamy sauce which is neither dry nor soupy.

In Italy, risotto is used mainly as a first course, like pasta, although there are occasional exceptions, as when it accompanies a meat dish like Osso Buco. Among Americans, it is just as often served (again, like pasta) as a main dish in a lighter meal, especially when it is dressed up with seafood, meats, or poultry.

The following basic recipe applies to all the risotto recipes in this book, so familiarize yourself with it before starting on the individual recipes. The right kind of rice is as essential as the technique. Authentic Italian Arborio rice, a short-grain variety grown in the Po Valley, has exactly the right starch content to produce the unique texture of risotto. In Italy there are several grades of Arborio rice, but the best grade, Superfino, is as far as I know the only one available in the United States.

Because risotto takes a good 25 to 30 minutes of closely watched cooking, it is more suited to the home kitchen than to the schedules of busy restaurants. Like many other restaurants, we use an interrupted method that allows us to precook the risotto until it is about 90 percent done then finish it to order in a little over 5 minutes. It's a shortcut that can also help busy home cooks. Take the Grilled Lamb Chops on page 132 and their accompanying eggplant risotto, for example. Unless your stove and grill are right next to each other, it's difficult to attend to both the chops and the risotto at the same time; and the fire may not be ready to grill the chops at just the right time to match the risotto. Using the interrupted method, you can grill the chops and let them rest on a heated platter while you put the finishing touches on the rice.

BASIC
RISOTTO TECHNIQUE

Stock (chicken, veal, or shrimp)
Olive oil
Minced shallots and garlic
Arborio rice
Salt

1. Bring the stock to a simmer in a saucepan; have a large ladle at hand. Heat the oil over medium heat in a large, heavy saucepan, preferably one that is wider than it is deep. Add the shallots and garlic to the pan and cook until they are soft but not browned. Add the rice and cook, stirring, until it is evenly coated with oil. Ladle in enough stock to cover the rice by about ¼ inch (2½ to 3 cups for 2 cups of rice). Cook, stirring frequently and scraping the bottom and sides of the pan, until the liquid is nearly absorbed (when the level of the liquid drops below the surface by about the thickness of a grain of rice).

2. Add another cup or so of stock and cook, stirring frequently, until it is nearly absorbed. Keep adding stock a cup at a time and cooking until it is nearly absorbed. After adding about 5 cups of stock in all, taste a grain of rice. When only a touch of crunchy raw texture remains in the center, the rice is about 90 percent done.

3. Add another cup or so of stock and the salt to the rice. Some recipes call for a sauteed mixture to be cooked separately at this point; in others, ingredients such as mushrooms are added to the risotto to cook along with the rice. After the final addition of liquid and whatever other ingredients are called for, cook the risotto until the liquid is nearly absorbed and only a thick "gravy" remains. Taste for seasoning and for doneness; each grain should be fully cooked but still slightly firm in the center, like *al dente* pasta.

Variation: *Interrupted Method*
If you cannot prepare the risotto from start to finish at one time, steps 1 and 2 can be done a few hours to 2 days ahead. When the rice is 90 percent done, pour it into a shallow baking pan in a layer no more than ¾ inch thick. Set it aside to cool at room temperature; cover and refrigerate if storing the risotto for more than about 2 hours. Finishing the dish is a simple matter of adding the cooked rice to a pan with the other cooked ingredients and the last addition of stock, wine, or other liquids. Depending on how dry the risotto has become, anywhere from 1 to 2 cups of additional liquid will be needed at this point.

SAFFRON RISOTTO
WITH SCALLOPS
AND SHRIMP

Saffron and rice is a classic combination, as is saffron and seafood. The three come together in this dish, an Italian cousin to the Spanish *paella*. If a whole teaspoon of saffron threads seems like a lot, that's intentional. I find that many dishes made with saffron have the right color but not much of the distinctive flavor of this expensive spice. In this dish you definitely taste the saffron.

Serves 4

> 6 to 7 cups Chicken Stock (page 34) or shrimp stock (see Note)
> 1 teaspoon (loosely packed) saffron threads
> 3 tablespoons olive oil
> 2 tablespoons minced shallots
> 1 tablespoon minced garlic
> 1 pound (2 cups) Arborio rice
> 2 teaspoons salt
> ½ pound raw shrimp, peeled, deveined, and butterflied
> ½ pound scallops
> 1 cup dry white wine
> 2 tablespoons butter
> 3 tablespoons chopped reconstituted sun-dried tomatoes (see page 35)
> ⅓ cup fresh basil leaves, coarsely chopped

1. Please read the Basic Risotto Technique on page 91 before beginning this recipe. Bring the stock to a simmer in a saucepan and have a large ladle at hand. Place the saffron threads in a large, heavy saucepan, preferably one that is wider than it is deep. Crush them with the back of a metal spoon. Add 2 tablespoons of the oil and stir with a wooden spoon over medium heat until the oil begins to stain yellow. Set aside 2 teaspoons of the shallots and 1 teaspoon of the garlic and add the rest to the pan along with the rice. Cook, stirring, until the rice is evenly coated with the yellow oil. Continue cooking according to the Basic Technique until the rice is about 90 percent done (through step 2).

2. Add another cup or so of stock and the salt to the rice. While it cooks, combine the remaining oil, shallots, and garlic in a large skillet. Cook over high heat until soft and fragrant; add the shrimp and scallops. Cook until they are halfway opaque, then add the wine and bring to a boil.

3. Add the contents of the skillet to the risotto. Stir in the butter, tomatoes, and basil and cook until the liquid is nearly absorbed and only a thick "gravy" remains. Taste for seasoning and for doneness; each grain should be fully cooked but still slightly firm in the center, like *al dente* pasta.

Variation: If you cannot prepare the risotto from start to finish at one time, step 1 can be done ahead (see Variation: Interrupted Method, page 91). When you are ready to continue with step 2, cook the seafood in the same pan used to cook the risotto, and add the partially cooked rice along with the wine. Depending on how dry the risotto has become, anywhere from 1 to 2 cups of additional stock will be needed at this point.

Note: Shrimp shells, tails, and heads (if they come with the heads attached) make a flavorful addition to the stock for this risotto. To make shrimp stock, heat a tablespoon of oil in a large saucepan and cook the shells and other trimmings until they turn red. Add about a cup of the same chopped vegetables and herbs as for Chicken Stock (page 34), cook briefly, and add about 2 quarts of chicken stock, or half stock and half water. Simmer 30 minutes to 1 hour and strain.

RISOTTO
WITH SMOKED CHICKEN
AND DRIED CHERRIES

There's nothing very traditional about this dish; it's typical of the way we rework traditional Italian dishes with the ingredients available here and now. Infusing the stock with the essence of the smoked chicken carries its flavor into every grain of rice. By itself, the smoked flavor can be a bit much, but the tartness of dried cherries brings it into balance and the almonds add a rounding, nutty flavor.

Like all the other risotti in this chapter, this is a rich and substantial dish. It's suitable for a first course, preferably to precede something without a lot of sauce; but it could just as well be a main dish for a lighter meal. Note that the first step takes about an hour of simmering time—you might want to bone the chicken and make the stock a day or two ahead.

Serves 4

- ½ smoked chicken (about 1½ pounds)
- 7 cups Chicken Stock (page 34)
- 2 tablespoons olive oil
- 2 tablespoons minced shallots
- 1 pound (2 cups) Arborio rice
  Salt and freshly ground pepper, to taste
- ⅓ cup dried cherries
- 3 tablespoons butter
- 2 tablespoons toasted slivered almonds

1. Skin the chicken and reserve the skin. Pull or cut the meat from the bones in as large pieces as possible. Discard any easily removable fat and cut about 12 ounces of the meat into bite-size pieces. Reserve any remaining meat for another use. Combine the skin and carcass, broken up as necessary to fit the pot, in a large saucepan with the stock. Bring it to a boil, skim, reduce the heat, and simmer 30 minutes to 1 hour.

Strain the stock, let it stand until the fat rises to the top, and skim off and discard the fat.

2. Please read the Basic Risotto Technique on page 91 before beginning this step. Return the smoked chicken stock to the pan and keep it at a simmer; have a large ladle at hand. Heat the oil in a large, heavy saucepan over medium heat. Add the shallots and rice and cook, stirring, until the rice is evenly coated with oil. Ladle in enough stock to cover the rice by about ¼ inch (2½ to 3 cups). Continue cooking according to the Basic Technique until the rice is about 90 percent done (through step 2).

3. Add another cup or so of stock to the rice and season to taste with salt and pepper, allowing for the saltiness of the smoked chicken. Add the chicken, cherries, and butter and cook until the rice is done and the liquid is nearly all absorbed. Serve immediately, garnished with the almonds.

Note: Hot-smoked chickens, which are cured in brine and then cooked in the smoking process, are available in some delis and specialty poultry markets. We use an applewood-smoked version made by Hobbs Shore in San Leandro, California, which is a bit milder in cure and smoke flavor than others. (I also use it because I like Hobbs a lot.) This kind of high-quality smoked product tends to come from small and locally distributed producers, so if his products are not available in your area, seek out other good local brands.

Variation: If you cannot prepare the risotto from start to finish at one time, you can use the interrupted method on page 91, adding the chicken, cherries, and butter with the last addition of stock. If you run short of the smoked chicken stock, ordinary chicken stock will do.

WILD MUSHROOM RISOTTO

Risotto is a great carrier for the flavor of any kind of mushrooms, but one or more of the wild mushroom varieties discussed on page 27 will make an especially memorable risotto. This dish, made with rich veal stock, is especially appropriate in autumn or early winter, when the greatest variety of wild mushrooms is available. Follow it with any roasted or grilled poultry or meat for a warming seasonal meal. If you have a hunter in the family, this is one of the best first courses to go with just about any kind of game.

Serves 3 to 4

> 3 cups (approximately) Brown Veal Stock (page 34)
> 3 tablespoons olive oil
> ½ pound chanterelles, hedgehogs, porcini, or other meaty wild mushrooms, sliced ¼ inch thick
> 2 tablespoons minced shallots
> 1 teaspoon minced garlic
> 1 cup Arborio rice
> Salt and freshly ground pepper, to taste
> 2 tablespoons butter

1. Please read the Basic Risotto Technique on page 91 before beginning this recipe. Bring the stock to a simmer in a large saucepan; have a large ladle at hand. Heat the oil in a large, shallow saucepan over high heat. Add the mushrooms and saute just until they begin to brown. Remove them with a slotted spoon and reduce the heat to medium. Add the shallots and garlic to the pan and cook until fragrant; do not brown. Stir in the rice and cook, stirring, until it is well coated with oil. Continue cooking according to the Basic Technique through the last addition of stock.

2. When the last addition of stock is nearly gone, return the mushrooms and their juices to the pan; add the butter. Taste for seasoning, adjust if necessary, and serve immediately.

Variation: If you can't get fresh wild mushrooms, dried porcini work every bit as well in this dish. Reconstitute them in water or stock, and be sure to add the soaking liquid (strained of any dirt and debris) to the broth used in cooking the risotto.

Even the more exotic cultivated varieties such as shiitakes and oyster mushrooms will make an extraordinary risotto. Try them singly or in com-bination with other wild or cultivated mushrooms.

Risotto
with Spring Vegetables

An assortment of spring vegetables gives fresh, sweet flavors and several different shades of green to this delightful risotto. Finish it off with a final drizzle of fragrant, emerald-colored pesto oil for a dramatic first course to precede any meat or fish entree.

Serves 4

> 7 cups Chicken Stock (page 34) or vegetable stock (see Note)
> 4 tablespoons olive oil
> 2 tablespoons minced shallots
> 1 pound (2 cups) Arborio rice
> 1 cup freshly shelled or frozen peas
> 1 cup diced asparagus
> 1 large leek, white and pale green parts, sliced crosswise (about 1 cup)
> 2 cups (loosely packed) spinach leaves
> Salt and freshly ground pepper, to taste
> 3 tablespoons unsalted butter
> 2 tablespoons oil skimmed from Pesto (see page 29)
> 1 ounce (approximately) shaved Parmesan cheese (see page 21)

1. Please read the Basic Risotto Technique on page 91 before beginning this step. Have the stock at a simmer and a large ladle at hand. Heat 2 tablespoons of the oil in a large, heavy saucepan over medium heat. Add the shallots and rice and cook, stirring, until the rice is evenly coated with oil. Ladle in enough stock to cover the rice by about ¼ inch (2½ to 3 cups). Continue cooking according to the Basic Technique until the rice is about 90 percent done (through step 2).

2. Heat the remaining oil in a skillet. Add the peas, asparagus, and leek and saute until they begin to soften. Add about a cup of stock and the spinach, bring to a boil, and season to taste. Add the vegetables to the risotto with the last addition of stock.

3. When the risotto is ready, season it to taste and stir in the butter. Serve on flat plates, with the pesto oil drizzled around the outside. Lay the shaved Parmesan on top and serve immediately.

Variation: If you cannot prepare the risotto from start to finish at one time, you can use the interrupted method on page 91, adding the vegetables and butter with the last addition of stock.

Note: If you want a completely vegetarian version of this dish, you can make a vegetable stock. Coarsely chop an assortment of vegetables and heat them gently in a little olive oil in a covered pan until they begin to "sweat." Add water to cover and an herb bouquet of parsley, thyme, and bay leaf and simmer 1 hour. Celery, carrots, and either onions or leeks are the essentials; whole garlic cloves, scrubbed unpeeled potatoes, and summer squash are nice additions. Cabbage should be used sparingly if at all, and avoid broccoli, cauliflower, or peppers. The trimmings of the vegetables in this risotto—the leek tops, the ends of the asparagus spears, and the hulls of the pea pods—all work fine.

SALADS AND SIDE DISHES

INSALATE E CONTORNI

MIXED GREENS WITH BALSAMIC VINAIGRETTE

BALSAMIC VINAIGRETTE

KULETO'S CAESAR SALAD

CAESAR DRESSING

SPINACH SALAD WITH PANCETTA AND MUSHROOMS

MEDITERRANEAN CHICKEN SALAD

SAUTEED SPINACH OR CHARD WITH PANCETTA

BALSAMIC ROASTED ONIONS

GRILLED NEW POTATOES

GRILLED POLENTA

CREAMY POLENTA WITH PARMESAN CHEESE AND ROSEMARY

TUSCAN-STYLE WHITE BEANS

ROASTED AND PEELED PEPPERS

The classic Italian *insalata* is a simple salad, full of the clean, bright flavors of greens and sometimes other vegetables, good olive oil, and a bit of vinegar. It's more often than not served after the entree, although Americans generally prefer salad early in the meal.

Also included in this chapter are a couple of more substantial salads suitable for lunch or supper entrees, plus a famous Italian-American, or more accurately Italian-Mexican, invention, the Caesar salad. They may not make this salad in Italy, but the combination of romaine, garlicky croutons, Parmesan cheese, and an anchovy-flavored dressing seems right at home in an American Italian restaurant. Follow it with a pasta and you have an ample meal.

Contorni literally means "contours," in the sense of giving contour to the entree, rounding it out. Strictly applied, it refers to the vegetables which go on the plate with the meat, poultry, or whatever constitutes the main dish. As used in restaurants here, it generally means vegetables served à la carte. Pasta and rice are never referred to as contorni on Italian menus, but we stretch the category slightly to include polenta, a popular side dish of cooked cornmeal.

I have placed the vegetable recipes in a separate chapter because that's how they appear on our menu, as à la carte selections. But most of them show up first as part of an entree. When composing daily specials or new additions to the menu, I don't consider an entree complete until I have added the right vegetable garnish. So in the entree recipes in the next chapter you will find more ideas for contorni, such as the grilled endives that accompany the grilled tuna on page 138. You will also find some recipes that incorporate side dishes from this chapter in entrees, as in the sauteed spinach garnish for Veal Scaloppine with Lemon, Capers, and Artichokes (page 129). Look back and forth between these two chapters for more ideas when composing menus.

Mixed Greens with Balsamic Vinaigrette

MIXED GREENS WITH BALSAMIC VINAIGRETTE

A mixed green salad should be just that—a mixture of greens, each offering a slightly different flavor, color, and texture. Starting with a base of one or more mild lettuce varieties such as butter or Bibb, red leaf or green leaf, I like to add an assortment of stronger greens to add bitter and peppery flavors: arugula, radicchio, Belgian endive, watercress, curly endive (chicory), kale, baby mustard greens, even some young tender dandelion leaves from the lawn. Some supermarkets and produce markets sell just such a mixture of greens (known in the business as "yuppie salad") for those who don't want to go to the trouble and expense of buying a bunch or a head of everything. Of course, if you grow an assortment of greens in your garden or even in a window box, you can assemble just the blend you want any time.

At home I mix the dressing for this kind of salad right in the bowl before adding the greens. If you prefer to make your balsamic vinaigrette in quantity, a recipe follows the main recipe.

Serves 4

> 2 tablespoons balsamic vinegar
> Pinch *each* salt and freshly ground pepper
> 1 teaspoon finely minced shallots or green onions (white part only)
> 1 small clove garlic, finely minced
> ½ teaspoon minced fresh tarragon
> 4 tablespoons extra virgin olive oil
> 6 ounces mixed salad greens, torn into bite-size pieces, washed and spun dry

1. Combine the vinegar, salt, and pepper in a large salad bowl and mix with a salad fork until the salt dissolves. Add the shallots, garlic, tarragon, and oil and mix until thoroughly blended. Dip a piece of lettuce in the dressing, shake off the excess, and taste; adjust the flavors to taste with more oil, vinegar, or seasonings if necessary.

2. If not serving the salad right away, set the dressing aside. Just before serving, stir the dressing again to mix the oil and vinegar. Add the greens to the bowl and toss until each leaf is lightly coated with dressing; serve immediately.

BALSAMIC VINAIGRETTE

At Kuleto's we make this dressing in quantity to use for various salads and antipasti. The sweet, round flavor of balsamic vinegar allows a higher proportion of vinegar than in dressings made with other vinegars. You can vary the herbs according to what is available, or to bring out a certain effect. For example, tarragon with tomatoes and basil with tomatoes are both good combinations, although they are quite different in flavor.

Makes ½ cup

>   2 teaspoons minced shallots or green onion (white part only)
> 1 small clove garlic, minced
> ⅓ cup extra virgin olive oil
>   Scant 3 tablespoons balsamic vinegar
> 1 teaspoon chopped fresh tarragon, basil, or dill
>   Scant ¼ teaspoon salt
>   Freshly ground black pepper, to taste

Chop the shallots and garlic together, then mash them slightly with the side of the knife blade (or combine them in a mortar and pound to a rough paste). Combine them with the remaining ingredients in a bowl or blender and whisk or blend until thoroughly mixed. Taste for seasoning and adjust if necessary. Store for up to a week in a tightly sealed jar; refrigerate if keeping for longer than overnight, but let it come to room temperature before serving. The dressing will separate as it stands, so whisk or shake well just before using.

Variation: If you can't get balsamic vinegar, or if you prefer a more conventional vinaigrette, use a good red wine vinegar in place of the balsamic vinegar. Remember that ordinary wine vinegar tastes more acid than balsamic, despite the fact that it is lower in actual acidity (see page 36). Start with 1½ to 2 tablespoons wine vinegar and adjust it to taste from there.

KULETO'S
CAESAR SALAD

Despite the name, Caesar salad did not originate in Rome, or even in Italy; it was invented in the 1920s by an Italian restaurateur in Tijuana, Mexico. Now it is on the menu of nearly every Italian restaurant in America, including this one. Here is our version.

Serves 4

    4 thick slices crusty white bread
    1 tablespoon olive oil
    1 teaspoon minced garlic
    1 teaspoon chopped parsley
    2 heads romaine lettuce
    ½ cup Caesar dressing (recipe follows)
    1 ounce Parmesan cheese
    4 anchovy filets (optional)

1. Tear the bread, including the crusts, into ½-inch cubes. Toss them in a bowl with the oil, garlic, and parsley and spread them on a sheet pan. Bake in a 350°F oven until crisp and lightly browned, about 15 minutes; let cool.

2. Remove the dark outer leaves from the romaine, leaving the pale green hearts. Trim the hearts to about 7 inches long, quarter each lengthwise, and slice each quarter across into pieces about 1½ inches wide. Place the pieces in a large salad bowl, drizzle with the dressing, and toss to coat the leaves evenly. Toss in the croutons and serve the salad on large plates. Shave thin slices of Parmesan onto each serving with a vegetable peeler, and garnish with a whole anchovy filet, if desired.

CAESAR DRESSING

At Kuleto's we use this dressing on Caesar salad and, in combination with pesto, in the grilled radicchio on page 50. It will keep in the refrigerator for a couple of weeks. If the oil begins to separate, just toss it back in the blender or processor to re-emulsify.

Makes 2 cups

> 3 large egg yolks
> 4 large oil-packed anchovy filets,
>   drained (see Note)
> 1 teaspoon minced garlic
> 1 tablespoon Dijon-style mustard
> 1 tablespoon Worcestershire sauce
> 1 tablespoon lemon juice
> 3 tablespoons grated Parmesan
>   cheese
> 1 teaspoon freshly ground black
>   pepper
> ¼ teaspoon salt
> 1¼ cups olive oil
> ¼ cup red wine vinegar

Combine all the ingredients except the oil and vinegar in a blender or food processor. Blend to a smooth paste. Add half the oil and half the vinegar and blend until smooth and well emulsified. With the motor running, add the remaining oil and vinegar and blend thoroughly. The dressing should be the consistency of lightly whipped cream.

Note: Good canned anchovies have firm, reddish filets that lift easily out of the oil without breaking and are not excessively salty. There is a lot of variation among brands, so shop around and if you find a favorite brand, stick with it. You might find anchovy paste (sold in tubes in well-stocked delis) a convenient substitute. Start with 1 teaspoon in place of the 4 filets and add more to taste.

SPINACH SALAD WITH PANCETTA AND MUSHROOMS

Wilted spinach salads with warm bacon dressings are so popular in the United States that we just had to come up with our own version. This is one of the best illustrations of the difference between pancetta, with its peppery and garlicky flavors, and the usual smoky American bacon.

Serves 4

  1 tablespoon olive oil
  3 ounces pancetta, diced
  1 tablespoon minced shallots
  1 teaspoon minced garlic
  2 tablespoons sherry vinegar
  1 tablespoon Dijon-style mustard
  1 tablespoon extra virgin olive oil
    Leaves from 1 large bunch spinach, washed and spun dry
  $\frac{1}{3}$ cup (1$\frac{1}{2}$ ounces) crumbled fresh goat cheese
  $\frac{1}{2}$ cup roasted and peeled red pepper (about 1 large pepper), cut or torn into strips
  $\frac{1}{4}$ cup toasted pine nuts
    Freshly ground pepper, to taste
  4 large Marinated Grilled Mushroom caps (see page 44), sliced in thirds

1. Heat the oil and pancetta together over medium-high heat and cook until crisp. Remove the pancetta with a slotted spoon and set it aside. Add the shallots and garlic to the pan and cook until fragrant. Remove from the heat and stir in the vinegar and mustard, then the extra virgin oil.

2. Place the spinach in a large bowl. Pour in the dressing and toss to coat the leaves. Add the remaining ingredients and the reserved pancetta. Toss lightly. When serving, arrange some of the pepper, cheese, pancetta, and pine nuts on top.

MEDITERRANEAN
CHICKEN SALAD

This is a more substantial salad than most, suitable as a cold entree for a light lunch or supper. You could also serve it as an antipasto, or a first course to precede a pasta.

Serves 4

½ frying chicken **OR** 2 pounds chicken parts

¼ cup *each* diced onion, carrot, and celery

Water or chicken stock

¼ pound green beans

2 ripe Roma tomatoes

OREGANO VINAIGRETTE
Juice of 1 lemon (about 2 tablespoons)

⅓ cup extra virgin olive oil

2 teaspoons minced shallots

½ teaspoon dried oregano

Salt and freshly ground pepper, to taste

4 cups mixed salad greens, including both mild and bitter

2 tablespoons capers

¼ pound aged ricotta cheese (see Note), crumbled

½ cup Marinated Olives (see page 41)

1 teaspoon dried oregano leaves

1. Place the chicken in a pot with the diced vegetables and add enough water or chicken stock to cover. Bring to a boil, skimming off any foam from the surface. Cover, turn off the heat, and let stand 45 minutes before removing the cover. Let the chicken cool in the liquid, then remove and chill it. (Save the broth as a thin chicken stock for making risotto or soup.)

2. Parboil the beans in lightly salted water until just tender. Transfer them to a bowl of ice water to stop the cooking; drain and cut into manageable lengths. Halve the tomatoes lengthwise, remove the cores, and slice the flesh lengthwise. Skin the chicken and remove the meat from the bones. Remove any fat and gristle and tear the meat by hand into long shreds.

3. Combine the vinaigrette ingredients in a large bowl and stir to dissolve the salt. Add the greens, chicken, beans, tomatoes, and capers and toss to coat evenly. Transfer to individual plates, top with the crumbled cheese and olives, and crumble a little oregano over each serving.

Note: The cheese we use in this salad, known in Italian as *ricotta salata moliterna*, is not to be confused with ordinary fresh ricotta. Like the fresh version, it is made from the whey left over from the manufacture of other cheeses, in this case from *pecorino* (sheep's milk) cheeses. Look for it in well-stocked cheese shops; if it is unavailable, substitute a mild feta such as the Corsican variety, which is somewhat similar in texture and flavor.

SAUTEED SPINACH OR CHARD WITH PANCETTA

It's hard to think of an entree — meat, poultry, or seafood — that this simple but delicious vegetable dish can't accompany. Spinach and chard, red or green, are interchangeable; use whichever looks better and is a better buy. The recipe also works well with the more bitter greens such as kale, collards, and mustard.

Serves 4

    1 large bunch spinach or Swiss chard
    1 tablespoon olive oil
    2 thin slices pancetta, diced (about 2 tablespoons)
    1 teaspoon minced garlic
    Salt and freshly ground pepper, to taste

1. If using spinach, tear the larger leaves away from the stems; leave the smallest leaves attached to their stems. If using chard, grab the leaves near the base and pull upward, stripping the leaves from the thicker part of their central rib. Wash the leaves well and drain them thoroughly in a colander or, better still, spin them dry in a salad spinner.

2. Combine the oil and diced pancetta in a large skillet over medium heat. Cook until well browned and slightly crisp. Add the garlic, cook for a few seconds, and add the spinach or chard. Cook, stirring and tossing, until the leaves are just wilted but still bright green. Taste for seasoning, tasting a bit of pancetta along with the greens; depending on how salty and peppery the cure, no more seasoning may be necessary. Serve immediately.

BALSAMIC ROASTED ONIONS

Roasting onions brings out their natural sweetness, which is further enhanced by the mellow sweetness of balsamic vinegar. These onions are a great accompaniment to most meats, poultry, or fish (see the Salmon with Red Wine–Olive Butter on page 142 for one particularly good match). Or serve them at room temperature as part of an antipasto plate with roasted peppers or cured meats.

Serves 4

    2 large or 3 medium red onions
    1 tablespoon olive oil (approximately)
    Salt and freshly ground pepper
    3 to 4 tablespoons balsamic vinegar

1. Preheat the oven to 350°F. Trim the roots off the onions, but leave the bases intact. Split the onions from root to stem end and cut each half into wedges (3 or 4, depending on size). Place them skin side down in a shallow baking dish and drizzle them with oil. Cover with a lid or aluminum foil and bake until soft nearly to the centers, 20 to 30 minutes.

2. Uncover, drizzle a little vinegar over each wedge, cover, and return to the oven for 10 minutes. Serve warm or at room temperature.

GRILLED NEW POTATOES

Grilling, particularly over a wood fire, gives an especially nice flavor to thin-skinned potatoes. Since they are partially cooked ahead of time, the potatoes can be finished on the grill alongside whatever other foods are being grilled.

Serves 4

    8 "creamer" size new potatoes, washed, unpeeled
    2 tablespoons olive oil
    Salt and freshly ground pepper
    2 to 3 tablespoons Herb Aioli (see page 18)

1. Preheat the oven to 400°F. Place the potatoes in a shallow baking dish; rub them with 1 tablespoon of oil and season them lightly with salt and pepper. Bake until just tender, about 30 minutes. Let cool. (This step can be done a day or more ahead of time; keep the cooked potatoes refrigerated.)

2. Split the potatoes lengthwise and lay 4 halves in a row on the cutting board, cut side down. Run a thin skewer horizontally through the middle of the potatoes. Repeat with the remaining potatoes, making 4 skewers in all.

3. Rub the potatoes, especially the cut sides, with a little more oil and sprinkle on a little more salt and pepper. Grill over a moderate fire, starting with the cut side down against the grill, until golden brown and slightly crisp on the surface, 3 to 5 minutes per side. Remove the potatoes from the skewers onto a plate and serve with a mound of Herb Aioli on the side, or place a skewer on each plate with a spoonful of aioli.

GRILLED POLENTA

Polenta, Italian-style coarse cornmeal cooked in water or stock, makes a fine foundation for all sorts of savory dishes. It's rather bland by itself, but that blandness makes it a perfect carrier for the full flavors of braised meats, cheeses, and other rich preparations. This is the traditional way of preparing polenta: it is boiled in plain water and allowed to cool until it "sets up," then it is cut into triangles or squares and grilled or sauteed.

Serves 4

>   2 cups water
> ½ cup polenta
> ½ teaspoon salt
> ½ cup grated Parmesan cheese
>   1 teaspoon olive oil

1. Bring the water to a boil in a large saucepan. Add the polenta in a thin stream, stirring constantly with a whisk. Cook over medium heat, stirring frequently and scraping the sides and bottom of the pot, until the mixture is thick and bubbly (think of the shots of bubbling molten lava in documentaries about volcanoes). Remove the pot from the heat and stir in the salt and cheese. Pour the mixture into a lightly oiled 8 × 8-inch baking pan and let it cool to room temperature (refrigerate if storing for more than a few hours).

2. Turn the cold polenta out onto a cutting board and cut it into four equal squares, then cut each square into two triangles. Oil the triangles lightly and grill them over a moderate fire, starting with the bumpy side down, until golden brown, about 3 minutes per side.

Variation: Instead of letting the polenta cool and reheating it, you can serve it right after boiling. Either spoon it directly from the pot onto plates, or pour it out onto a platter or, even more traditional, a board or marble slab. If it is cooked thick enough, it will stop short of the edge, and within a few minutes it can be cut into hot slices which will keep their shape.

Variation: Polenta can be varied by stirring in all sorts of savory ingredients. Try replacing the Parmesan cheese with crumbled Gorgonzola, or adding toasted pine nuts and chopped sun-dried tomatoes, or stirring in chopped basil or Pesto (see page 29) or other herbs (see the rosemary version which follows). Choose ingredients which harmonize with the rest of the dish without repeating.

Squares or other shapes of polenta are also good reheated with Marinara Sauce (page 26) or Pesto, or with a cheese such as Gorgonzola or Taleggio melted over them.

CREAMY POLENTA WITH PARMESAN CHEESE AND ROSEMARY

This is a richer version of polenta, cooked in stock, flavored with herbs, and enriched with a little cream and cheese. It's meant to be served hot and freshly cooked, and a little bit of it goes a long way. Its best use is as an accompaniment to plain grilled or roasted meats and poultry, but we have a few regular customers who like it in place of pasta, topped with a sauce such as the one on Penne with Lamb Sausage, Chard, and Ricotta (page 88).

Serves 4

    2½ cups unsalted chicken stock
    ½ cup polenta
    ¼ teaspoon salt
    ¼ cup cream
    ½ teaspoon minced fresh rosemary
    ¼ cup grated Parmesan cheese

Bring the stock to a boil in a large saucepan. Add the polenta in a thin stream, stirring constantly with a whisk. Cook over medium heat, stirring frequently and scraping the sides and bottom of the pot, until the mixture is thick and bubbly. Stir in the salt, cream, rosemary, and cheese and taste for seasoning. The polenta can be served immediately or kept warm in a hot water bath for up to 2 hours. Serve in shallow bowls if serving as a side dish or first course, or on the plate as a bed for grilled meats.

TUSCAN-STYLE WHITE BEANS

Cooked white beans are a staple in many parts of Italy, but especially in Tuscany. They show up in soups, salads, pasta dishes, and as *contorni*. Real imported Italian *cannellini* beans are available dried in some markets, but they are quite expensive. I find domestic small white beans (also called navy beans) or Great Northern beans a fine substitute. Another alternative is canned cannellini, which are handy to keep on hand in the pantry for use on short notice.

To serve the beans as a side dish, dress them up with some sauteed spinach or chard, or roasted pepper strips, or olives, or mushrooms, or fresh tomatoes . . . whatever is in season and fits within the overall menu.

Makes 4½ cups

2 cups small white beans
10 cups water
2 teaspoons salt
2 bay leaves

Inspect the beans and remove any broken or shriveled ones or any bits of dirt or gravel. Rinse the beans if they are at all dusty. Place them in a large pot with the water, salt, and bay leaves and bring it to a boil. Reduce the heat and simmer uncovered until the beans are tender but not mushy, 1½ to 2 hours depending on the age of the beans. Let the beans cool in their liquid.

Note: If you will be using the beans in a salad, or as part of another dish, drain them in a colander. Spread the beans in a shallow pan to cool, then cover and refrigerate.

ROASTED AND PEELED PEPPERS

A daily chore for the cooks at Kuleto's is to roast a large batch of sweet bell peppers on the wood-fired grill to use in meat, poultry, and fish entrees as well as antipasto dishes, salads, and pastas. Roasting loosens the waxy outer skin so it can be removed easily, and the wood fire gives an especially smoky flavor. You can do the same on a charcoal grill, under a broiler, on top of a gas burner, or even with a hand-held propane torch.

Sweet peppers (red, yellow, green, orange, in any combination)

1. Place the peppers directly on a grill over a hot wood or charcoal fire, or arrange them on a broiler pan about 4 inches from the heat. Turn the peppers as they roast until the skins are evenly blistered all over; they can get quite black, but try to avoid burning the flesh underneath. As the peppers are done, transfer them to a bowl, a large jar, or other container and cover so they steam slightly, which helps the skins loosen further.

2. When the peppers are cool enough to handle, peel off and discard the skins. Slit the peppers open lengthwise and remove the stems, seeds, and ribs. Cut the flesh into strips. Save any juices that have collected in the bowl and add them to the peppers to help keep them moist. Roasted peppers will keep in the refrigerator for up to a week.

POULTRY, MEATS, AND FISH

POLLAME, CARNE, E PESCE

Roast Duck with Dried Cherries and Grappa

Chicken Breast Stuffed with Herbed Ricotta

Grilled Chicken with Tuscan Bread Salad

Braised Rabbit with Lemon and Olives

Veal Scaloppine with Lemon, Capers, and Artichokes

Braised Veal Shanks

Grilled Lamb Chops with Fresh Tomato Sauce and Eggplant Risotto

Eggplant Risotto

Adriatic Fish Stew

Grilled Tuna with Red Endives

Grilled Skewered Shrimp

Salmon with Red Wine–Olive Butter

Fish Paillards with Dill Pesto and Mushrooms

Baked Fish with Pine Nut Crust

Like the rest of the menu at Kuleto's, the entrees reflect a combination of Italian traditions and contemporary American trends. Even when we do a traditional dish, we tend to interpret it our way. In Italy if you order veal scaloppine, that's what you get on the plate. Here, we offer a more complete combination of meat, vegetable, and sometimes starch. This is partly a matter of what American diners expect, but it's also my own preference. That doesn't mean we have to use the same tired old formula approach to plates — meat at six o'clock, starch at ten o'clock, vegetable at two o'clock. Instead, I try to conceive each entree plate as a whole, for instance adding artichoke hearts to veal piccata and serving it on a bed of sauteed spinach. This sometimes means reaching into other menu categories for the accompaniments. For instance, the Tuscan bread salad known as *panzanella* is used as a separate course in Italy, but we find it makes a great accompaniment on the plate with grilled chicken.

The grill is a prominent feature of this chapter, as it is in our kitchen, but most of the grilled dishes can be adapted to an indoor stove-top grill or even the broiler. You might want to use a heavier hand with the seasonings and marinades when cooking under the broiler, as broiling can never give quite as much flavor to meat or fish as cooking over a fire.

ROAST DUCK
WITH DRIED CHERRIES
AND GRAPPA

Duck and fruit—either oranges or cherries—is a classic flavor combination that was introduced into French cuisine from Tuscany. It only works well for me if the sauce is not too sweet. I like to use tart dried cherries (see page 21) to balance the richness of the duck and the reduced veal stock that is the base of the sauce. A touch of grappa and orange liqueur rounds out the flavor.

Although this dish can be prepared entirely in a little over three hours, it's much more convenient to make the stock and do the preliminary roasting of the duck in advance, either earlier in the day or a day or two ahead of time. The final reheating and assembly can be done in about 10 minutes, less time than it takes to cook the polenta and cabbage.

Serves 4

　2 ducklings
　½ cup *each* coarsely chopped carrot, onion, and celery
　3 to 4 cups chicken stock
　½ cup balsamic vinegar
　1 tablespoon honey
　4 tablespoons oil
　½ red onion, thinly sliced
　½ head red cabbage, thinly sliced
　2 teaspoons caraway seeds, ground or crushed
　1 recipe Creamy Polenta (see page 113), without the rosemary but seasoned generously with coarsely cracked black pepper
　2 teaspoons minced shallots

　1½ ounces grappa (see Note) or other brandy
　1½ ounces Grand Marnier
　½ cup pitted dried cherries
　2 tablespoons butter
　　Salt and freshly ground pepper, to taste

1. Preheat the oven to 350°F. Remove the legs from the ducks, taking as much of the meat around the hip joints as possible. Remove the breasts whole, keeping the two halves together on the breastbone. Remove the wings for another purpose, if desired. Roughly chop the carcasses and place them in a roasting pan with the carrot, onion, and celery. Roast until well browned, about 1 hour, then transfer to a stock pot. Drain as much fat as possible from the roasting pan and deglaze the pan with a cup or so of the stock. Pour the contents of the pan into the stock pot, scraping in all the browned bits from the bottom. Add the rest of the stock and simmer 2 hours.

2. While the stock simmers, wash and dry the roasting pan and oil it lightly. Combine ¼ cup of the vinegar with the honey and brush the mixture on the skin side of the duck legs and breasts. Arrange them skin side up in the roasting pan and roast until the breasts are medium rare, about 30 minutes. Remove the breasts, cover the pan with foil, reduce the heat to 300°F, and continue cooking the legs until the meat shrinks back from the bones and is quite tender, another 45 minutes. Meanwhile, divide the breasts and remove the breastbones, making four boneless halves with skin attached. (Both the duck and the stock can be prepared to this point 2 to 3 days ahead of time and refrigerated.)

3. For the cabbage, heat 2 tablespoons of oil in a skillet over medium heat. Add the onion and cook until tender. Add the cabbage and caraway, cover, and simmer over low heat, stirring occasionally, until quite tender, about 45 minutes to 1 hour. While the cabbage cooks, prepare the Creamy Polenta and keep it warm. When the cabbage is tender, stir in the remaining ¼ cup of vinegar and season to taste. Keep warm.

4. Heat your largest skillet over medium-high heat and add enough oil to generously coat the bottom. Add as many duck pieces as will fit, skin side down, and brown them well. Turn and brown them on the other side. As the duck pieces are done, transfer them to a warmed platter. When all the pieces are browned, remove the skillet from the heat, discard the fat, and let the pan cool slightly, then add the shallots, grappa, and Grand Marnier. Let the mixture bubble in the pan for a few seconds, then touch a long lighted match to the pan to burn off the alcohol. Add 2 cups of the duck-flavored stock and return the pan to the heat. Bring it to a boil, return the duck pieces to the pan, and cook over high heat until the duck is heated through, about 5 minutes.

5. Make a bed of cabbage on one side of each plate and spoon polenta on the other side; place a duck leg in the center. Slice a breast half diagonally and fan the slices out across the plate, overlapping both cabbage and polenta. Return all the pan juices to the skillet, add the cherries, and reduce slightly. Swirl in the butter. Season the sauce to taste and spoon it over the duck.

Note: *Grappa* is an Italian brandy made from pomace, what remains of grapes after the wine has been pressed out of them. Like any brandy, it comes in various grades, from young and harsh to some expensive versions mellowed with age. The French equivalent is called *marc*. I'm not sure I would go out and buy a bottle of grappa just for this recipe, especially if I had some other decent brandy on hand.

CHICKEN BREAST STUFFED WITH HERBED RICOTTA

This is another dish that has been on the menu at Kuleto's from the beginning, and one that we couldn't retire even if we wanted to. The creamy filling of ricotta studded with dried tomatoes, herbs, and garlic makes it a warm and satisfying dish, and roasted peppers add a beautiful splash of bright color. Add a few slices of grilled eggplant or some sauteed spinach and you have a delicious lunch or dinner entree.

Serves 4

 1 cup ricotta cheese
 3 tablespoons chopped reconstituted sun-dried tomatoes
 2 tablespoons chopped basil
 2 teaspoons chopped chives
 2 teaspoons chopped fresh oregano
 2 teaspoons minced garlic
 Salt and freshly ground pepper
 4 (8-ounce) chicken breast halves, with upper wing joints attached (see Note)
 2 tablespoons olive oil
 Flour for dredging
 2 teaspoons minced shallots
 ⅓ cup dry white wine
 1½ cups sliced roasted and peeled peppers (red, yellow, or a combination)
 4 to 5 tablespoons unsalted butter
 12 long chives, for garnish

1. In a mixing bowl combine the ricotta, tomatoes, herbs, and 1 teaspoon of garlic; season to taste with salt and pepper. With a small knife make a 1-inch slit in each breast near the wing, insert the knife, and cut a triangular pocket in the meat to within an inch of the edges of the breast. Using a pastry bag or a small spoon, stuff each breast with a quarter of the ricotta mixture. (The chicken may be prepared to this point several hours ahead of time and refrigerated.)

2. Preheat the oven to 425°F. Heat the oil in a large skillet. Season the chicken breasts with salt and pepper and dredge them in flour, shaking off the excess. Brown them well on the skin side, then turn them and brown the skinless side. Transfer the chicken to a baking dish, skin side up, and bake uncovered until the meat is opaque, 15 to 18 minutes.

3. Transfer the breasts to a serving platter or individual plates. Pour off any excess oil from the skillet and saute the shallots and remaining garlic until soft. Discard any fat in the baking pan and deglaze the pan with the wine; scrape the contents into the skillet. Reduce the mixture by half, stir in the peppers, remove the skillet from the heat, and swirl in the butter. Season the sauce to taste and spoon it over the chicken. Garnish with long chives.

Note: The cut of chicken called for in this and the following recipe is a half breast with the upper wing joint still attached, but otherwise boneless (what the French call a *suprême*).

GRILLED CHICKEN WITH
TUSCAN BREAD SALAD

Panzanella, a Tuscan tomato and bread salad, is usually served on its own as a cold dish. Here its bright, slightly vinegary flavor provides a refreshing balance to the creamy sauce on the chicken. If you are really watching calories I suppose you could eliminate the sauce.

Serves 4

> 2 cups Brown Veal Stock or Chicken Stock (page 34)
> ¾ cup cream
> 4 teaspoons whole-grain prepared mustard
> 4 chicken breast halves, with upper wing joints attached (see Note, page 122)
> 4 chicken legs
> Salt and freshly ground pepper
> 4 ounces (about a 6-inch square) Focaccia (see page 22), cut into 1-inch cubes
> ¾ cup Champagne Vinaigrette (see page 59)
> 2 large tomatoes, coarsely diced
> 3 cups (loosely packed) arugula leaves
> 1 cup thinly sliced red onion

1. Combine the stock, cream, and mustard in a skillet or shallow saucepan. Bring to a boil, reduce by two-thirds, and set aside.

2. Season the chicken pieces lightly with salt and pepper and grill them until the juices run clear when pierced with a fork (see Technique Note). While the chicken cooks, place the bread cubes in a large salad bowl and toss them with half the vinaigrette. Set them aside for a few minutes, then add the tomatoes, arugula, and onion, the remaining dressing, and a pinch of salt and pepper and toss to combine. Divide the salad among four large plates. When the chicken is done, arrange one breast and one leg on top of each salad. Drizzle the mustard sauce over the chicken and serve.

Technique Note: Chicken legs take much longer to grill than boned breasts, which can make the timing of this dish tricky in a restaurant. At home it presents no problem. A covered grill works best. Start the legs first, cook them about halfway, and move them to the edge of the fire while you cook the breasts on the hottest part of the fire. Be sure to use the cover to prevent flare-ups that could char the skin. If all you have is an open grill, follow the same general plan, but cook the legs the whole way on the cooler part of the fire. You can also cook the chicken under an indoor broiler. Again, allow more time for the legs, and cook them a little farther from the heat if your broiler height is adjustable. For that matter, roast chicken would also be delicious served with *panzanella*.

BRAISED RABBIT
WITH LEMON AND OLIVES

Both rabbit (*coniglio*) and hare (*lepre*) are common in Italy. Hare is larger, darker, and gamier, while rabbit, especially a young farm-raised rabbit, has tender, mild-tasting white meat. In fact, rabbit cooks and tastes a lot like chicken, and it is usually sold in poultry shops in the United States.

This dish is a recent addition to the menu at Kuleto's. It will work with any variety of lemon, but it's especially good with Meyer lemons, the very fragrant, slightly orange-colored variety which is being grown in increasing quantities in California. They are easiest to find in the market in late winter and spring.

Serves 4 to 6

> 2 rabbits, about 2½ pounds each
> ½ pound *cipolline* or pearl onions, roots trimmed (see Note)
> 3 to 4 tablespoons olive oil
> 3 or 4 sprigs fresh thyme
> Salt and freshly ground pepper, to taste
> 1½ cups dry white wine
> 2 cups Chicken Stock (page 34)
> ½ cup *each* coarsely diced carrot, celery, and onion
> 1 bay leaf
> ½ pound mushrooms, halved or quartered if large
> 1 tablespoon *each* minced shallots and garlic
> ½ cup green olives, pitted
> 1 small lemon, halved lengthwise and sliced about ⅛ inch thick

1. To cut up the rabbits, remove the front legs along with the shoulder blades, then remove the hind legs, getting as much of the muscle around the hip joint as possible. Cut along each side of the backbone to separate the loin muscles, which run the full length of the backbone on either side. Carefully peel and cut the loins away from the ribs, taking the flap of breast meat along with each half. Remove the kidneys from their sheath of fat in the belly cavity and set aside with the livers, if desired. Save the carcasses for the stockpot.

2. Preheat the oven to 325°F. If using *cipolline*, peel them and cut them in half through the root end. If using pearl onions, peel them and leave them whole. Place them in a small foil-lined pan, drizzle with a bit of olive oil, add a sprig of thyme, and wrap them in the foil. Place the onions in the oven to start baking while you prepare and cook the rabbit. Remove them when tender, 45 minutes to 1 hour.

3. Heat 2 tablespoons of the oil in a large skillet. Season the rabbit parts all over with salt and pepper. Add the loins and brown them well on both sides over medium-high heat; remove and set aside. If using the livers and kidneys, brown them well and set aside with the loins. Add the legs to the pan and brown them well on both sides. As the legs are done, transfer them to a large baking dish. Add the wine and stock to the skillet and deglaze the bottom. Pour the contents of the skillet into the baking dish and add the diced vegetables, the remaining thyme, and the bay leaf. (If your skillet is large enough and has a tight-fitting lid, you can leave the rabbit legs in the skillet and use it for the baking dish.) Cover the dish and place it in the oven until the legs are tender, about 1 hour.

4. When the legs are nearly done, heat another tablespoon or 2 of oil in a skillet and saute the mushrooms with the shallots and garlic. Add the rabbit loins and giblets to the pan to reheat. Remove the baking pan from the oven and transfer all the rabbit pieces to a warm serving platter. Strain the sauce from the baking pan into the skillet and discard the braising vegetables. Add the olives and roasted *cipolline*, taste for seasoning, and correct if necessary. At the last minute, add the lemon slices just to warm them through. Transfer the contents of the skillet to the serving platter.

Note: *Cipolline* are miniature flat yellow onions 2 to 3 inches in diameter. They are not widely available, but pearl or boiling onions can be substituted. If none of these is available, use small round onions, cut through the root end into quarters.

128

Veal Scaloppine with Lemon, Capers, and Artichokes

I like to add quartered artichokes to the classic veal piccata, and to serve it on a bed of spinach. When artichokes are scarce and expensive, you can substitute dried tomatoes (see Variation).

Only pale pink, milk-fed Eastern veal gives the right combination of tenderness and flavor for this dish. The best cut of veal for scaloppine is the loin, but it's very expensive. Sirloin cuts are also a possibility. The traditional cut is the large muscle from the inside round on the leg, which needs more pounding to be tender. Cross-cut slices of turkey breast are also a good alternative. For that matter, pork loin makes very good scaloppine.

Serves 4

    12 veal scaloppine, 1½ ounces each,
        pounded ⅛ inch thick
       Salt and freshly ground pepper
       Flour for dredging
     3 tablespoons olive oil (approximately)
     2 teaspoons minced garlic
     4 tablespoons capers
    16 cooked artichoke quarters (see
        Note)
    ⅔ cup dry white wine
     4 teaspoons lemon juice
       Leaves from 1½ pounds spinach,
        washed and spun dry
     4 tablespoons butter (room temperature)

1. Season the scaloppine lightly with salt and pepper. Dredge them in flour and shake off the excess.

2. Heat a large skillet over high heat and add enough oil to generously coat the bottom. Add half the scaloppine (or as many as will fit in a single layer) and cook until lightly browned, about 45 seconds per side. Remove the first batch when browned on both sides and set aside on a warm plate. Add a little more oil and add the rest of the scaloppine. Immediately after turning, add the garlic, capers, artichokes, wine, and lemon juice. Bring to a boil, return the rest of the scaloppine to the pan, and reduce the sauce slightly.

3. Meanwhile, heat 1½ tablespoons of oil in another skillet and add the spinach. Cook until evenly wilted and season to taste with salt and pepper. Place a small mound of spinach in the center of each of four dinner plates.

4. Add a pinch of salt to the skillet with the veal and swirl in the butter. Lay three scaloppine on each plate, leaning them against the spinach. Divide the artichokes and capers among the plates and spoon the sauce over all.

Note: The marinated artichokes on page 42 will work fine in this dish, if you already have some on hand. If preparing them just for this dish, trim and cook them in the same way, but skip the marinating step. Or, you can use canned imported artichoke hearts, well drained, or even marinated hearts, drained and rinsed.

Variation: To serve family style, make a long mound of spinach in the middle of a large oval platter; arrange the scaloppine around the outside and top with the sauce as described above.

Variation: Omit the capers and artichokes in step 2, adding instead ⅓ cup reconstituted sun-dried tomatoes and 1 tablespoon each chopped fresh sage and parsley.

BRAISED VEAL SHANKS
——— OSSO BUCO ———

This is a hearty dish for cold weather. The meaty veal stock, the natural gelatin that cooks out of the shanks, and a full-bodied red wine combine to make a rich and flavorful sauce. To match its rustic style I like a garnish of beans and vegetables cut rather large, rather than the finely diced vegetables of a more classic presentation. I would serve it with a big red wine, say a Barolo, Brunello di Montalcino, or California Cabernet or Merlot.

Pale, milk-fed Eastern veal may be preferable for scaloppine, but this dish actually works better with the somewhat darker, more mature, "beefier" veal typical of the Western states.

Serves 4

    4 center-cut veal shanks (about 1
        pound each)
    Salt and freshly ground pepper
    Flour for dusting
    3 to 4 tablespoons olive oil
    1 cup *each* diced onion, celery, and
        carrots
    6 to 8 cloves garlic, roughly chopped
    2 cups red wine (see Wines for Cook-
        ing, page 36)
    3 cups Brown Veal Stock (page 34)
    2 bay leaves
    6 ounces *orecchiette* or other small
        dried pasta
    ½ large red onion, sliced vertically
        (stem to root)
    4 large leaves red or green chard, cut
        into 2-inch squares
    ¼ cup cooked white beans (see page
        115)

1. Preheat the oven to 400°F. Scrape off any light pink bone dust from the butcher's saw remaining on the shanks. Season the meat lightly with salt and pepper. Dust the cut surfaces of the meat with flour and shake off the excess. Heat a large skillet over medium-high heat and add oil to coat the bottom generously. Add as many of the shanks as will fit comfortably and brown them well on both sides. As they are done, transfer them to a deep baking pan.

2. When there is room in the skillet along with the last of the shanks, add the diced vegetables and garlic and cook until nicely browned. Transfer the last of the shanks to the baking pan, if you haven't already done so. Pour the wine and as much stock as will fit into the skillet and bring it to a boil, stirring to scrape up all the browned bits. Add the contents of the skillet to the baking pan, add the bay leaves, cover, and bake until the meat is quite tender, about 1½ hours. While the shanks braise, boil the pasta in salted water until just barely done, drain, rinse with cold water to stop the cooking, and oil lightly.

3. Remove the pan from the oven and transfer the shanks with a slotted spoon to a warm platter. Cover loosely with foil to keep them warm. Strain the braising liquid, let it stand until the fat rises to the surface, and skim off and discard the fat.

4. Meanwhile, heat 1 tablespoon of oil in a skillet and saute the red onion until soft. Add the chard and beans and cook until the chard begins to wilt. Add 3 cups of the defatted braising liquid, bring to a boil, and reduce by a third. Taste for seasoning and correct if necessary; stir in the cooked pasta to reheat. Pour the sauce over the shanks and arrange the vegetables and pasta all around.

Variation: Omit the pasta and serve the shanks on a bed of soft polenta (see Variation, page 112) or plain white risotto (see page 91).

Variation: The possibilities for vegetable garnishes are almost limitless. Try cooked artichokes (see page 42), dry-cured black olives, sun-dried tomatoes, blanched whole garlic cloves, mushrooms.

Variation: Braised Lamb Shanks
Use 4 whole lamb shanks (no need to have them cut crosswise) in place of the veal shanks. Follow the same cooking procedure and timing as for Osso Buco, but omit the pasta and the vegetable garnish. Instead, simply reduce the braising liquid to about 2 cups, add 1 cup of seeded and diced tomato to the reduced liquid, and swirl in 2 tablespoons of butter at the last minute. Serve on polenta or risotto, and for an optional but delicious garnish, drizzle each portion with a tablespoonful of Pesto (see page 29) made with half basil and half mint leaves.

GRILLED LAMB CHOPS WITH FRESH TOMATO SAUCE AND EGGPLANT RISOTTO

━━━━━━━━━━━━━━━━━━

Try this dish in late summer or early fall, when tomatoes and eggplant are at their best. We use T-bone chops from the lamb loin, but thick rib chops will also work.

Serves 4

> 8 loin lamb chops, about 1 inch thick
>   Salt and freshly ground pepper
> ½ cup extra virgin olive oil
> 3 cloves garlic, crushed
> 1 teaspoon fresh rosemary leaves
>   Eggplant Risotto (recipe follows)
>   **FRESH TOMATO SAUCE**
> 1¼ pounds ripe tomatoes
> ½ cup extra virgin olive oil
> 2 tablespoons minced shallots
> 1 tablespoon minced garlic
> 1 teaspoon *each* minced tarragon and rosemary
> 1 tablespoon balsamic vinegar
>   Salt and freshly ground pepper, to taste

1. Place the chops in a bowl, season them with a little salt and pepper, sprinkle generously with oil, and scatter in the garlic and rosemary. Marinate 2 hours.

2. Prepare the eggplant risotto through Step 1 (see Note). While the risotto cooks, prepare the tomato sauce as follows: Peel, seed, and coarsely chop the tomatoes and drain them well. Heat the oil in a deep skillet until it begins to smoke. Remove it from the heat and add the shallots and garlic. Let it stand about 15 seconds, stirring or shaking the pan, then add the tomatoes and herbs. Return the pan to the heat and cook 1 minute. Remove it from the heat, add the vinegar, and season to taste with salt and pepper.

3. Preheat the grill or broiler. Remove the chops from their marinade and grill or broil them to the desired degree of doneness, 6 to 8 minutes for medium rare. Meanwhile, finish cooking the risotto with the eggplant. Spoon the risotto into the center of each plate or a serving platter, arrange the chops on top, and surround them with the tomato sauce.

EGGPLANT RISOTTO

3 to 4 cups Chicken Stock (page 34)
3 tablespoons olive oil
½ medium eggplant, peeled and cut in
⅜-inch dice (about 1 cup)
2 tablespoons minced shallots
1 teaspoon minced garlic
1 cup Arborio rice
Salt and freshly ground pepper, to
taste
2 tablespoons unsalted butter

1. Please read the Basic Risotto Technique on page 91 before beginning this recipe. Bring the stock to a simmer in a saucepan; have a large ladle at hand. Heat 2 tablespoons of oil in a heavy saucepan over medium-high heat. Add the eggplant and saute it until lightly browned. Remove it with a slotted spoon and set it aside. Add the remaining oil to the pan; add the shallots and garlic and cook until soft but not browned. Stir in the rice and cook until the rice is evenly coated with oil. Ladle in enough stock to cover the rice by about ¼ inch and cook, stirring frequently and scraping the bottom and sides of the pot, until the liquid is nearly absorbed (when the level of the liquid drops below the surface by about the thickness of a grain of rice). Add another ladleful of stock and cook until it is nearly absorbed. Keep adding stock a ladleful at a time and cooking until nearly absorbed. After adding about 2½ cups in all, taste a grain of rice; only a touch of crunchy raw texture should remain in the center. (If it needs more cooking to get to that point, add more stock and cook down again.)

2. Stir in the eggplant and add stock to cover again, season to taste, and cook until the liquid is nearly absorbed and all the rice grains are done.

Note: Timing can be a little tricky as you try to get the charcoal fire, the risotto, and the chops all synchronized. The two-stage risotto cooking process described on page 91 can really help here. If you make the risotto all at once, start cooking the chops just a little before you add the eggplant to the risotto. (Be sure you have allowed enough time for the fire to reach the perfect cooking stage.) If you want to play it safe, start grilling the chops a little earlier; they can stand to rest a few minutes before serving, but the risotto should be served immediately once it is ready.

Variation: Grill a butterflied leg of lamb (it cooks in about 45 minutes in a covered grill), carve it, and serve it with the same sauce and risotto.

ADRIATIC FISH STEW
——— BRODETTO ———

Italy has a lot of coastline, and wherever there are fish there is likely to be a fish soup or stew called *brodetto*. Every region has its own versions, most with tomato, a few without. Like many versions from the Adriatic coast, this one calls for both red wine and a little vinegar.

The recipe here is just a guide, not a fixed formula. This is not a dish to plan way ahead of time, but a way to take advantage of a good day at the fish market. Chances are slim that you will find all the fish and shellfish items listed here on any given day, so keep your ideas flexible. Just remember to try for an assortment of shellfish and firm, meaty fish such as those listed below. Most markets that cut up their own fish (rather than buying it already fileted and portioned) have some odds and ends of various fish. These tail sections, belly trimmings, and meat from the heads should sell for a good deal less than the perfect steaks lined up on trays in the display case. If you shop early in the day, you may even get your choice of varieties among the "chowder chunks."

Serves 4

    2 tablespoons extra virgin olive oil
    1 cup diced onion
    1 tablespoon minced garlic
    2 tablespoons minced parsley
    5 cups peeled and seeded tomatoes,
        with juice
    1 cup not-too-tannic red wine
    2 tablespoons red wine vinegar

    ¾ teaspoon kosher salt
        Pinch of red pepper flakes
    1 tablespoon *each* chopped basil and
        tarragon
    8 small clams
    16 mussels or live scallops in the shell
    ½ pound monkfish filet
    ½ pound swordfish steak, about ½
        inch thick
    8 large shrimp
    2 pounds squid, cleaned, sacs cut
        into rings (see page 55)

1. Heat the oil in a large saucepan or dutch oven. Add the onion and saute until soft. Add the garlic and parsley and cook another minute or two, until the onion begins to color. Break the tomatoes apart by hand and add them to the pan with their juice. Add the wine, vinegar, salt, and pepper flakes. Simmer until slightly reduced, 10 to 15 minutes. Add the chopped herbs in the last couple of minutes. (The sauce can be made to this point several days ahead of time and refrigerated, or set aside at room temperature for a few hours.)

2. Meanwhile, prepare the fish and shellfish. Scrub the clam, mussel, and scallop shells well to remove any grit; pull the beards off the mussels. Remove any transparent membrane from the monkfish filet and slice it crosswise into ¾-inch rounds. Cut the swordfish into 4 equal pieces. Slit open the shrimp shells on the outer and inner curves, split the meat almost to the tail end, and remove the veins.

3. Bring the tomato sauce to a boil and add the clams and monkfish. Cover and adjust the heat to maintain a lively simmer. After 3 minutes, add the swordfish. One to 2 minutes later add the mussels or scallops and shrimp. Replace the cover after each addition. Cook until the mussels open and the fish appears done. Transfer the cooked fish and shellfish to warm shallow bowls. Clams sometimes take a long time to open, so if necessary, return them to the simmering sauce. Add the squid and cook just until it turns opaque, about 30 seconds. Divide the sauce and squid among the bowls and serve immediately.

Note: When live clams and mussels are cooked, some of them spread wide open quickly while others barely crack open. The latter can be pried open with a spoon or tongs, but the really stubborn ones that never open even a crack may be dead, so it's safest to discard them.

GRILLED TUNA
WITH RED ENDIVES

Italian cooks have many varieties of endive (chicory) to choose among. For a long time the only variety available in the U.S. was the yellowish-white Belgian endive, but now we can also get several of its Italian cousins. I like to combine it with the similarly shaped but fuller-flavored red *radicchio di Treviso* as a grilled vegetable to accompany fish or meats. This dish will work equally well with other meaty, full-flavored fish such as swordfish, albacore, and other tunas.

Serves 4

> 1 large red onion
> 2 tablespoons olive oil
> 1 teaspoon fresh thyme leaves
> ½ cup Balsamic Vinaigrette (page 103)
>   Salt and freshly ground pepper, to taste
> 1 head *radicchio di Treviso*
> 2 heads red or white Belgian endive
> 4 yellowfin tuna steaks, 5 to 8 ounces each

1. Peel the onion and split it vertically (stem to root). Cut each half crosswise into ¼-inch slices. Heat 1 tablespoon of the oil in a skillet over medium-low heat. Saute the onion gently, stirring frequently, until it is soft and lightly browned. Stir in the thyme and add balsamic vinaigrette to taste (about 2 tablespoons). Season to taste with salt and pepper and keep warm.

2. Prepare a charcoal fire with hotter and cooler parts. Quarter the Treviso lengthwise, leaving a piece of root attached to each quarter. Split the Belgian endives in half. Drizzle all the cut surfaces with the remaining vinaigrette, letting it run down between the leaves. Moisten the tuna steaks with a little oil and season them with salt and pepper. Start the vegetables cooking on the hotter part of the fire; brown them quickly on all sides, then move them to the cooler side to finish cooking. Grill the fish on the hottest part of the fire to the desired degree of doneness, about 2 minutes per side for rare, 3 to 4 minutes for medium. Serve each portion of tuna with the two types of endive and spoon the onion mixture partially over both fish and vegetables.

139

GRILLED
SKEWERED SHRIMP

This can be done with any large or jumbo shrimp. The largest sizes (generally called prawns on the West Coast) typically come from Mexico or the Gulf Coast; at 10 to 12 to the pound, 3 or 4 of them make an ample and impressive serving. When we can get them, we like to use the large fresh spot prawns from central California or Alaska. Of course, smaller shrimp will be just as delicious cooked this way; just remember that they take less time to cook. Note that the shrimp marinate overnight.

Serves 4

1⅓ pounds large or jumbo raw shrimp

  MARINADE
  1 cup olive oil
  Grated zest of 3 oranges
  ⅓ cup orange juice
  ⅔ cup lemon juice
  2 teaspoons minced garlic
  2 teaspoons minced parsley
  1 to 2 teaspoons red pepper flakes
  1 teaspoon salt, or to taste

4 Belgian endives, split lengthwise
  Olive oil, for brushing
  Salt and freshly ground pepper
2 red or yellow peppers, roasted,
    peeled, and sliced

1. With small scissors or cutting *outward* with a paring knife, slit the shell of each shrimp down the length of the back to expose the intestinal tube (vein); remove the veins. Carefully pull the meat loose from the shell, leaving it attached at the tail end, then put it back inside (this helps make the shrimp easier to peel after cooking). Rinse the shrimp well and drain thoroughly.

2. Lay out one portion of shrimp on the table, lined up in the same direction. Pass one thin skewer through all the shrimp near the head ends, and another parallel to the first near the tail ends. Repeat with the remaining portions. Lay the shrimp in a container which will hold them snugly. Combine the marinade ingredients and pour half the marinade over the shrimp. Cover and refrigerate the shrimp and the remaining marinade (which will be the sauce for the finished shrimp) overnight.

3. Prepare a medium-hot fire and preheat the grill thoroughly. Drain the shrimp and discard their marinade. Let the reserved sauce come to room temperature. Brush the endive halves with a little oil, season them lightly, and grill until lightly browned on both sides; set them aside near the edge of the grill. Grill the shrimp until the meat is opaque white, 2 to 3 minutes per side. With the largest sizes, it helps to pull them off the skewers when they are about two-thirds done and put them on the grill with the open sides down to finish cooking.

4. Arrange the endives on one side of each plate. Remove the shrimp from the skewers and arrange them with tails inward on the other side of the plate. Place a small pile of roasted peppers in the center and drizzle the sauce over all.

141

SALMON WITH
RED WINE–OLIVE BUTTER

Although salmon is not found anywhere near Italy, it is *the* prestige fish on the West Coast of the United States, and Italian restaurants here feature it just as often as other restaurants. Salmon and red wine is no longer the novel combination it once seemed. The rich flavor of the fish, especially a Pacific king salmon, goes wonderfully with a not-too-tannic red wine, such as Pinot Noir or most Merlots, as well as with the robust flavor of black olives.

Serves 4

> Balsamic Roasted Onions (page 111)
> 4 diagonal slices skinless salmon filet,
>   5 to 6 ounces each
> Salt and freshly ground pepper
> 4 tablespoons olive oil
> ¼ cup minced shallots
> 1½ cups sliced mushrooms
> 1½ cups coarsely chopped chard leaves
> ½ cup red wine
> ¼ cup Chicken Stock (page 34)
> 1 teaspoon lemon juice
> ½ cup pitted and halved Kalamata
>   olives
> ¼ pound unsalted butter, in 1-table-
>   spoon pieces

1. Prepare the onions and keep them warm. Season the salmon lightly on both sides with salt and pepper. Heat 2 tablespoons of the oil in a medium skillet and add the shallots; cook a few seconds, then add the mushrooms, chard, and a pinch of salt and pepper; saute until tender. Arrange the sauteed vegetables in the center of 4 warm dinner plates.

2. Meanwhile, heat the remaining oil in another large skillet to near smoking and add the salmon, skin side up. Cook until well browned on the first side, turn, and cook until the fish just begins to flake around the thin edges. If for some reason the salmon is done before the vegetables, remove it from the heat. Otherwise, lay the salmon portions on top of the vegetables as soon as they are done.

3. Return the vegetable pan to the heat and add the wine, stock, lemon juice, and olives. Bring the mixture to a boil and reduce it by half. Add the butter and swirl the pan or stir with a whisk until the butter is all melted and incorporated into the sauce. Taste the sauce for seasoning and spoon it over the salmon. Surround each serving with 2 or 3 onion wedges.

Note: Cooking the salmon in one skillet and the vegetables and sauce in another and making the whole thing come out together is second nature to restaurant cooks. If the timing seems tricky, just remember that it is better for the vegetables to wait a little while for the salmon than vice versa. The sauce does not keep very well, so it's best to time it to be done at the same time as the fish. If stovetop space is a problem, you could broil the salmon, eliminating one burner and skillet.

FISH PAILLARDS WITH DILL PESTO AND MUSHROOMS

I believe that fish paillards, thin cuts of fish pounded so thin they can cook directly on the plate, were introduced into Bay Area restaurant cooking by Jeremiah Tower at Stars. They have caught on because they cook quickly, make a modest portion of fish appear to go farther, and provide a large platform for sauces and other toppings. They make just as much sense for the home cook; here is an entree that cooks so quickly you can enjoy a first course with your dinner guests, then slip into the kitchen and whip up the entree in less than five minutes.

This dish will work with any fine-textured, moderate to rich fish, such as salmon, sea bass, redfish, sea trout (weakfish), or striped bass, to name a few. It will also work with a wide variety of wild and cultivated mushrooms, although I think ordinary button mushrooms are kind of boring in this case.

Serves 4

> 4 diagonal slices skinless fish filet, 4 to 5 ounces each (see Technique Note)
> 2 tablespoons olive oil, plus more for rubbing
> ½ pound black or golden chanterelles, oyster mushrooms, or fresh shiitake mushrooms
> Salt and freshly ground pepper, to taste
> ¾ cup Pesto (page 29), made with dill in place of basil and without cheese

1. Lightly rub the surface of a piece of fish with oil. Place it between two plastic bags and pound it carefully with a mallet or the side of a cleaver to a thickness of a little less than ¼ inch. Set aside and repeat with the remaining portions. (The fish may be pounded several hours ahead of time and refrigerated; use cooking parchment or plastic wrap to separate the portions, and remove them from the refrigerator at least 5 minutes before cooking.)

2. Prepare the mushrooms according to their density: leave black chanterelles whole; slice golden chanterelles ¼ inch thick, shiitakes a little thinner; leave small oyster mushrooms whole, cut the larger ones in half.

3. Preheat the broiler, or preheat the oven to 500°F. Lay the fish portions out on 4 heatproof dinner plates. Season them with salt and pepper and spread each with an even layer of pesto.

4. Heat the oil in a skillet and start the mushrooms cooking over high heat. Place the fish plates under the broiler or in the oven. Cook just until the fish is turning opaque all over, about 1½ to 2 minutes. Remove the plates from the oven, season the mushrooms to taste, and spoon them over the fish. Serve immediately.

Technique Note: Cutting a large filet (such as one from a good-sized salmon) on a diagonal produces a single slice that pounds down to a paillard easily. If your fish is smaller, or is cut on less of a diagonal, it may be better to allow two slices per serving. In either case, the starting thickness should be no more than ½ inch.

BAKED FISH
WITH PINE NUT CRUST

A crunchy topping of bread crumbs and pine nuts bound to the fish with a pungent black olive paste makes this dish a favorite whenever it appears on the menu. We crumble the croutons from our Caesar salad (see page 104) for the bread crumbs, which gives an extra bit of flavor, but that's optional. Any leftover olive paste is delicious spread on toast as an appetizer.

Serves 4

   3 tablespoons pine nuts
   ½ cup dry seasoned bread crumbs or seasoned croutons
   ¼ cup Kalamata olives, pitted
   1 teaspoon minced shallots
   1 teaspoon minced garlic
   ½ teaspoon lemon zest
   1 teaspoon minced fresh tarragon
   2 tablespoons olive oil
   Salt and freshly ground pepper, to taste
   4 filet portions halibut, sea bass, cod, or other firm white fish, 5 to 6 ounces each
   Juice of 1 lemon
   ¼ cup (approximately) dry white wine
   1 cup julienne onions or leeks
   Leaves from ½ pound fresh spinach
   1 cup peeled, seeded, and chopped tomatoes

1. Chop the pine nuts fairly fine by hand or in a food processor and mix them with the bread crumbs. (If using croutons, chop them and the pine nuts together to coarse crumbs.) Set aside.

2. Combine the olives, shallots, garlic, lemon zest, and tarragon on a cutting board and chop them finely together. Transfer them to a bowl and stir in enough olive oil to make a spreadable paste; season to taste.

3. Preheat the oven to 450°F. Lightly oil a baking dish just large enough to hold the fish. Spread one side of each fish portion with about 2 teaspoons of the olive paste and lightly press a quarter of the crumb mixture on top. Place the fish in the baking dish crumb side up and carefully pour the lemon juice and wine around the fish to a depth of about ⅛ inch. Bake uncovered until the fish is tender in the center when probed with a skewer, 6 to 10 minutes depending on the variety of fish and the thickness of the cut.

4. While the fish is baking, heat 2 tablespoons of oil in a large skillet and saute the onions until soft. Add the spinach and tomatoes and cook until the spinach wilts. Season to taste and arrange on warm plates; top with the baked fish.

DESSERTS

DOLCI

TIRAMISÚ

ANISE AND ALMOND BISCOTTI

HAZELNUT BUTTER COOKIES

WILD CHERRY AND ALMOND COOKIES

ZABAGLIONE

SEMIFREDDO

CHOCOLATE BREAD PUDDING

CHOCOLATE BREAD

HAZELNUT CUSTARD

LEMON AND WHITE CHOCOLATE SORBETTO

Dessert is not a traditional part of an Italian meal; Italians tend to take their sweets between meals, often in cafés. But restaurant customers here expect dessert, and our pastry chef Denise Mondot is happy to oblige with everything from a simple plate of cookies to a knockout Semifreddo (a frozen layered mousse) or Tiramisú, the Italian answer to the English trifle.

Just as ingredients such as olive oil, tomatoes, garlic, and Parmesan cheese recur in many Italian savory dishes, the most typical Italian sweets are based on a limited number of flavors that come up again and again in different combinations: almonds, hazelnuts, anise seeds, citrus fruits, cherries, and chocolate. In this chapter you will find them used in traditional ways, as well as in such newer combinations as a lemon sorbet enriched with white chocolate.

The more elaborate desserts are probably something you will prepare only for company, but a simpler dessert like Zabaglione or Hazelnut Custard can be just the thing to dress up a weekday family meal. The various kinds of cookies (*biscotti*) are easy to make and keep well in a cookie jar, so make a batch when you have a few extra minutes and keep them on hand for late-night snacks or whenever friends come by for coffee.

TIRAMISÚ

The Italian name of this rich, creamy cousin of the English trifle means "pick me up," no doubt in reference to the amount of rum and coffee involved. A fairly recent addition to the Italian *pasticciere*'s repertoire, it has quickly become one of the most popular desserts at Kuleto's, and many other Italian restaurants. Our version is a little firmer than most, intended for unmolding and serving in slices rather than spooning out of the serving dish, as is more typical.

Serves 6 to 8

> 3 tablespoons cake flour
> Scant 5 tablespoons cornstarch
> 3 large eggs, separated
> 1 cup plus 4½ tablespoons granulated sugar
> ½ cup plus 1 tablespoon dark rum (Myers's or another top-quality brand)
> 4 teaspoons instant espresso powder
> 1 pound Italian mascarpone (see page 20)
> ½ cup confectioner's sugar
> 1 cup cream
> 1 teaspoon pure vanilla extract
> ½ cup grated bittersweet chocolate
> 3 tablespoons half-and-half

1. **Ladyfinger Cake:** Preheat the oven to 350°F. Lightly grease a 9 × 13-inch jelly roll pan, or coat it with nonstick cooking spray. Line the bottom of the pan with baking parchment and grease the top of the parchment as well. Sift the flour and cornstarch together.

2. Place the egg yolks in a mixing bowl with 4 teaspoons of sugar; beat with a hand mixer or the whisk attachment of a tabletop mixer until the mixture forms a slowly dissolving ribbon when it falls from the beater. Set aside. With a clean whisk or beaters beat the egg whites until foamy, then sprinkle in 2½ tablespoons of sugar. Continue beating until the mixture holds stiff but not dry peaks.

3. Transfer the yolk mixture to a large bowl and sprinkle the flour mixture over it; stir with a few quick strokes of a large rubber spatula just until lightly blended (there should still be some unmixed flour at this point). Add about a quarter of the egg white mixture and stir until well blended. Fold in the rest of the whites gently; avoid overmixing or the cake will be heavy.

4. Spread the batter in an even layer in the prepared cake pan, filling the pan all the way to the corners. Bake until the cake is lightly browned and begins to shrink from the sides of the pan, 6 to 8 minutes. Let cool in the pan.

(continued)

5. **Espresso Syrup:** Combine 1 cup of the sugar and 5 fluid ounces of water in a saucepan. Bring to a boil, simmer until the sugar is all dissolved, and remove from the heat. Let cool slightly, then stir in 3 ounces of rum and the espresso powder. Set aside to cool thoroughly.

6. **Filling:** Combine ¾ pound of mascarpone and the confectioner's sugar in a large mixing bowl. Beat just until the mixture has some body (don't overmix or the butterfat and water may separate). Stop and scrape the bowl once or twice during mixing. Combine the cream, vanilla, and 2 tablespoons of rum in another mixing bowl. Beat to the stiff-peak stage. (If you have an electric mixer, you can use it to beat the mascarpone, transfer it to the larger bowl, and whip the cream in the same bowl used for the mascarpone. There's no need to clean it.) Stir a third of the whipped cream into the mascarpone mixture, then fold in the rest. Cover and refrigerate.

7. Cut a sheet of parchment to line an 8½ × 4½-inch loaf pan (see illustration). Trim the edges of the cake and cut three rectangles to match the size of the pan. Lay a piece of cake in the pan upside down and drizzle it with espresso syrup until saturated. Spread it with a layer of filling equal to the thickness of the cake. Repeat with another layer of cake, another dousing of syrup, another layer of filling, and one more layer of cake. Moisten again with syrup. Wrap tightly and chill overnight. Wrap and chill the remaining filling.

8. An hour or two before serving, invert the Tiramisú onto a serving dish and remove the parchment. Stir the remaining filling until smooth and spread it evenly over the top and sides. Grate a generous layer of chocolate over the top and chill until ready to serve. Combine the remaining mascarpone with 1 tablespoon each sugar and rum; beat until light, then add the half-and-half and beat to a smooth, pourable consistency. Chill. To serve, slice the Tiramisú crosswise and stand each slice on a plate. Spoon a little of the mascarpone topping over and around each portion.

Variation: Tiramisú is traditionally made and presented in a glass bowl, to be scooped out with a spoon rather than inverted and sliced (see photo). To make it in a bowl, skip the step of lining the dish with parchment, cut the cake to fit the shape of the bowl, and instead of wrapping and chilling the remaining filling in step 7, spread it on top. Reserve the grated chocolate to sprinkle over each serving.

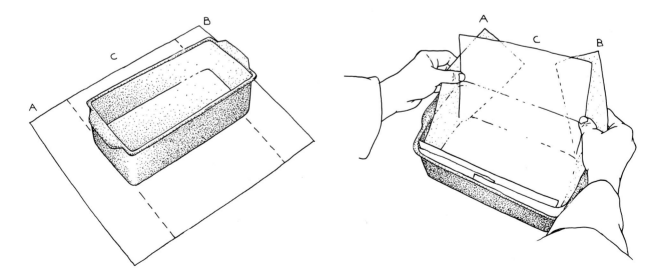

ANISE AND ALMOND
BISCOTTI

These cookies are an all-time Italian classic. The word *biscotti* literally means twice cooked, and is the root of our word biscuit. Baking them twice results in a hard, dry cookie — too hard to eat dry, but that's just the point. They are meant to be dunked in coffee, or even more typically in a sweet wine such as Vin Santo, Spumante, or port.

Makes 6 dozen

- ¼ pound unsalted butter (room temperature)
- 1½ cups sugar, plus more for dusting
- 2 tablespoons whole anise seeds
- 2 teaspoons ground anise seeds
- 3 large eggs
- 1 teaspoon pure vanilla extract
- 3¾ cups all-purpose flour
- 1 tablespoon baking powder
- ½ teaspoon salt
- 1 cup whole almonds

1. Preheat the oven to 325°F. Cream the butter, sugar, and both kinds of anise with a hand mixer or the paddle attachment of a tabletop mixer until light and fluffy. Break the eggs into a bowl or pitcher, add the vanilla, and add gradually to the butter mixture. Combine the dry ingredients and add them in a thin stream; mix just until the dough comes together. If using a heavy-duty mixer, you can add the almonds along with the flour, otherwise stir them in after the dough comes together.

2. Line two 11 × 17-inch baking pans with parchment. Sprinkle your work surface with a teaspoon or so of sugar. Divide the dough in thirds and with your hands roll each third into a 15-inch log, being careful to work out any air pockets. Lay two of the logs well apart on one pan, the third on the other pan. Bake until firm and golden brown, about 45 minutes. The rolls will spread considerably as they bake, becoming long, flat ovals in cross section.

3. As soon as the rolls come out of the oven, reduce the heat to the lowest setting it will hold, preferably 175°F or lower. (If you want to proceed right away, leave the oven door open for a few minutes to get the temperature down.) Transfer each roll to a cutting board and slice it diagonally into 24 pieces about ½ inch thick. Slip a long knife under the row of slices and transfer it back to the same paper-lined pan on which it was baked. Push the slices alternately left and right, leaving them standing up and just touching in the center so they support one another. Return the pans to the oven until the cookies are thoroughly dry and crisp, about 1½ hours. Let them cool in the pan then store them in a cookie jar or other airtight container for up to 10 days.

HAZELNUT BUTTER
COOKIES

▬ ▭ ▬ ▭ ▬

Substitute *pasta nocciole* (hazelnut butter) for the peanut butter and you have a very Italian interpretation of the all-American peanut butter cookie. A whole hazelnut pressed into the top of each cookie adds an elegant touch to these tender, just slightly chewy cookies.

Makes 4 dozen

> ½ cup brown sugar
> ½ cup granulated sugar, plus more for rolling
> ½ cup unsalted butter (room temperature)
> 1 cup all-purpose flour
> ½ teaspoon salt
> ½ teaspoon baking soda
> 1 large egg
> 1 cup hazelnut butter (see Note)
> 1 teaspoon pure vanilla extract
> 48 whole hazelnuts, toasted and skinned (see Note)

1. Cream the sugars and butter together at high speed until light and fluffy. Blend the dry ingredients together. Stir the egg, hazelnut butter, and vanilla into the butter and sugar until evenly mixed. Add the dry mixture and mix gently just until the flour is absorbed. Spread the dough on a sheet of parchment or foil, mixing it a little more as you spread it. Wrap it tightly and chill 4 hours to overnight.

2. Preheat the oven to 375°F. Put some sugar in a bowl. Form the dough into 1-inch balls. As it is formed, drop each ball into the sugar, roll it around, and shake off the excess sugar. Place the balls 2 inches apart on parchment-lined cookie sheets. Press a nut well into the top of each ball, flattening it slightly. Bake until just slightly browned on the bottom, about 10 minutes. Let the cookies cool about 5 minutes in the pans, then transfer them to a cooling rack. Store in an airtight container for up to 10 days.

Note: We use imported Italian hazelnut paste (*pasta nocciole*), but it may be hard to find outside a professional baker's supply. You may find domestic hazelnut butter in health food stores; to substitute for the Italian, it should be made from toasted, not raw, nuts. To make your own, toast and skin whole hazelnuts (see below) then grind them to a paste in a food processor. Be patient; even with the high-speed motor of the processor it takes several minutes to go from finely chopped nuts to a smooth paste. Store whatever form of hazelnut butter you use tightly sealed in the refrigerator.

To skin hazelnuts, spread the whole nuts (often sold as filberts) on a sheet pan and toast them in a 350°F oven until fragrant and light golden in the center (crack one open to see), 6 to 8 minutes. While still warm, transfer the nuts to a clean, dry kitchen towel, fold the towel over, and rub vigorously to remove the skins. Pick out the skinned nuts as you go and continue working the rest until the nuts are all or nearly all skinned.

WILD CHERRY AND ALMOND COOKIES

These very Italian cookies will appeal to lovers of macaroons and marzipan. At the heart of each ball of almond paste is a whole preserved cherry, specifically the dark red, slightly bitter variety known as *marasche* or *amarene*. We buy these cherries, packed in syrup in large cans imported from Italy, from a commercial baker's supply. They can be found in jars in well-stocked Italian delis, but they are quite expensive. You might see if an Italian bakery in your area uses them in bulk and could sell you a small amount. I suppose you could make the cookies with other canned cherries, but they won't taste exactly the same.

Makes 24

    12 ounces unsweetened almond paste
    1 large egg white
    ¼ teaspoon orange extract OR grated zest of ½ orange
    4 cups (approximately) sliced almonds
    24 preserved wild cherries

1. Combine the almond paste, egg white, and orange extract or zest in a mixing bowl and beat with the paddle attachment of an electric mixer or a spoon to a light, loose texture.

2. Preheat the oven to 325°F. Spread the sliced almonds in a shallow pan; line a baking sheet with parchment. Dip your hands in a small bowl of water to moisten them well, and pinch off a heaping tablespoon of dough. Form it into a thick disc, place a cherry in the center, and form the dough into a ball around the cherry, enclosing it as evenly as possible. Drop the ball onto the sliced almonds. Repeat, making 24 balls in all.

3. Dry your hands. Pick up a ball and some sliced almonds; roll the ball in your palms, gently pressing the almonds into the surface until it is evenly coated. The balls get slightly deformed in the process, so gently shape them back into spheres before placing them on the lined baking sheet.

4. Bake the cookies until lightly browned, 12 to 15 minutes. Let them cool completely before serving.

ZABAGLIONE

This wine-flavored foam of eggs and sugar is a perfect choice when you want a sweet but light ending to a meal. You can serve it in a fancy cookie cup (*tuile*), in a parfait glass, or layered in a bowl with fresh berries.

Marsala, a sweet fortified Sicilian wine, is the traditional wine for making zabaglione, but you can use a wide variety of wines. The more distinctive the fruity character of the wine, the more it will come through in the finished dish. At Kuleto's we use Quady Essencia, a delicious and lightly fortified Orange Muscat wine from California. Other strong Muscat wines from Italy, Spain, France, and California are another option, as are lower-alcohol Muscats of the *amabile* and sparkling Asti Spumante styles. Also Riesling, Champagne . . . the possibilities are almost endless.

Serves 6 to 8

> 1 cup cream
> 5 large egg yolks
> 6 tablespoons sugar
> ¾ cup sweet white wine (see choices above)
> Raspberries, strawberries, or other fresh fruit (optional)

1. Whip the cream until stiff but not dry; cover and refrigerate. Combine the egg yolks, sugar, and wine in a large stainless or heatproof glass bowl. Set the bowl over boiling water and beat with a large wire whisk until the mixture is thick and foamy and it has more than doubled in volume. Be sure to whisk all parts of the bottom and sides of the bowl regularly, to avoid clumps of "scrambled-egg" texture. The texture is right when the whisk drawn quickly through the whole mass leaves a valley which takes a second or two to fill back in. Depending on the level of heat, the whole process may take 10 minutes or more of steady beating.

2. **To cool with a tabletop mixer:** Immediately transfer the mixture to the mixer bowl and beat with the whisk attachment at medium-high speed. Fill a shallow bowl with cracked ice and slide it in under the mixer bowl, raising it as necessary so the ice is in contact with the mixer bowl. Continue beating until the mixture is tepid. **By hand:** Place the bowl containing the cooked egg mixture inside a larger bowl of cracked ice and beat steadily until the mixture is tepid.

3. Beating slowly (low speed on an electric mixer), add the whipped cream in large spoonfuls. Beat until evenly blended, then chill until ready to serve. Zabaglione will keep up to 2 days in the refrigerator; if it begins to thin out, you can whip it again and add a little more whipped cream for additional stability. To serve, spoon over fresh fruit in parfait glasses or other glass dishes.

Technique Note: There really is no substitute for a strong arm and a wire whisk in making zabaglione. The first step, whipping the egg mixture over the heat, must be done by hand. The cooling stage in step 2 can be done in a tabletop mixer with a bowl of ice slipped underneath the mixing bowl.

For the sake of simplicity, the instructions here call for whipping the cream first. However, if you have a tabletop mixer, you could whip the cream at the same time as you are cooking the egg mixture. Having a second bowl for the mixer is handy so you don't have to stop and clean the bowl before the cooling stage.

SEMIFREDDO

This intensely flavored dessert is for chocolate lovers. Desserts don't get much richer than this one, so you might be tempted to skip the sauce. Don't! The combination of lightly soured cream and unsweetened espresso is just what is needed to balance the other sweet, rich flavors.

Serves 16

> 6¼ cups cream
> ¼ cup buttermilk
> 2 pounds bittersweet chocolate
> 2½ cups sugar
> 24 large egg yolks
> ½ cup cake flour
> 6 tablespoons cornstarch
> 6 tablespoons liquid espresso extract OR 6 tablespoons instant espresso powder dissolved in 2 scant tablespoons vanilla
> Cocoa powder
> 16 thin chocolate cutouts (optional)

1. **At least 24 hours ahead of serving,** combine 2 cups of the cream and the buttermilk in the top of a double boiler and warm them to 100°F. Remove from the heat, transfer to a clean, warm glass container, cover, and let stand overnight at warm room temperature.

2. **Eight to 24 hours ahead of serving,** make a baked chocolate mousse as follows: Preheat the oven to 350°F. Grease or spray a 10-inch springform pan and line the bottom with a circle of baking parchment; line the sides with a strip of parchment at least 3 inches wide. Chop 1 pound of the chocolate coarsely and melt it over hot (not boiling) water. Set aside to cool slightly. Meanwhile, beat 1¼ cups of cream and ½ cup of sugar to soft peaks in a chilled bowl; set aside.

3. Combine 12 egg yolks and ¾ cup sugar in a large mixing bowl and beat until the mixture is pale yellow and forms a slowly dissolving ribbon when the beater is lifted. Sift the flour and corn- starch together, add them to the yolk mixture, and mix at medium speed just until the dry ingre- dients are incorporated. Stir a quarter of the whipped cream into the melted chocolate, then fold in the rest. Add a quarter of the yolk mix- ture, stir until well blended, and fold in the rest. Transfer the mixture to the prepared baking pan and set the pan inside a roasting pan. Place the pans in the oven and pour hot water into the outer pan to come up about ½ inch around the sides of the springform pan. Bake until the cake is nearly set but a skewer inserted in the center still comes out sticky, about 1 hour. Let cool thoroughly in the pan.

4. When the cake is thoroughly cooled, make an espresso mousse as follows: Chop the remaining 1 pound of chocolate coarsely and melt it over hot (not boiling) water. Meanwhile, combine the remaining 3 cups of cream with ½ cup sugar and 3 tablespoons of espresso extract in a chilled bowl and beat to soft peaks; set aside. Combine the remaining 12 egg yolks and ¾ cup of sugar in a large mixing bowl and beat to the ribbon stage. Add the whipped cream and the yolk mixture to the chocolate in the same sequence as in step 3 (stir in a small portion first, then fold in the rest). Straighten up the parchment around the sides of the cake pan to make a complete collar, then spread the uncooked mousse mixture in an even layer on top. Place the cake in the freezer until firmly frozen, at least 8 hours. While it is freez- ing, combine the ripened cream and the remain- ing 3 tablespoons of espresso extract.

5. To serve, remove the sides of the pan and the paper collar. Slice the cake with a sharp knife, wiping the blade clean with a damp towel be- tween cuts. Serve on large plates, each spread with about 2 tablespoons of the espresso-flavored cream. Dust the slices with a little cocoa pow- der. Garnish the tops with decorative shapes cut out of a sheet of melted and cooled chocolate.

CHOCOLATE BREAD PUDDING

There are certainly sweet bread puddings and chocolate breads made in Italy, but I am pretty sure that putting the two together in a chocolate bread pudding is an American invention. There's certainly nothing Italian about the cranberries in the sauce either, but I like the way they go with chocolate, especially in the company of orange zest and liqueur. We have also served this pudding with a rich nutmeg cream sauce and drizzled with a little chocolate sauce. It's also delicious with just a scoop of vanilla ice cream.

Serves 10 to 12

> 4 ounces bittersweet chocolate, coarsely chopped
> 3 cups cream
> Scant 3 tablespoons flour
> ¾ cup plus 1 teaspoon sugar
> 1½ teaspoons *each* ground nutmeg and cinnamon
> 4 large eggs
> 1 braided or oblong loaf Chocolate Bread (recipe follows)
>
> **CRANBERRY AND ORANGE COMPOTE**
> 2 cups water
> 3 cups sugar
> 4 cups fresh or frozen cranberries
> Grated zest of 3 oranges, in long julienne strips if possible
> ¼ cup Grand Marnier
> ½ cinnamon stick

1. Combine the chocolate and 1 cup of the cream in a heatproof bowl or the top of a double boiler. Warm over boiling water just until the chocolate is all melted; meanwhile, combine the dry ingredients in another large bowl. Remove the chocolate bowl from the heat and stir in the eggs, then the remaining cream. Pour over the dry ingredients and stir with a whisk until well blended.

2. Preheat the oven to 325°F. Slice the bread a little less than ½ inch thick. Lightly butter an 9 × 13-inch baking pan and fill it with two rows of overlapping slices, in opposite directions if you like. The slices should overlap by about half their width so they come up to the full height of the pan. If holes remain in the corners, fill in with smaller or partial slices.

3. Pour the chocolate custard mixture evenly over the bread, moistening every slice. Place the pan in a larger roasting pan, put them in the oven, and add hot water to the outer pan to half the depth of the pudding pan. Bake until a knife inserted in the center comes out clean, 35 to 45 minutes.

4. While the bread pudding cools, combine the compote ingredients in a saucepan and bring them to a boil. Reduce the heat to low and simmer until the berries are soft but not shriveled, 10 to 15 minutes. Remove the mixture from the pan. Strain the liquid back into the pan and boil it down until it is reduced by half. Remove the pan from the heat, discard the cinnamon stick, and return the berries to the syrup. Serve the bread pudding warm (1 to 2 hours out of the oven is just right) with warm compote spooned around each serving.

CHOCOLATE BREAD

Besides being used in the bread pudding above, this is a popular breakfast bread in Italy. Although the pudding recipe calls for only one loaf, it takes no more time or trouble to make a full recipe. Then you can make either two loaves or one loaf and a batch of rolls (see variation).

Makes 2 loaves

> 3¼ cups bread flour or all-purpose flour, plus more for dusting
> Scant 3 tablespoons unsweetened cocoa
> ½ ounce fresh yeast, crumbled (see Note, page 25)
> 1½ tablespoons cold unsalted butter, diced
> 1½ tablespoons mild olive oil
> 2 tablespoons sugar, plus more for sprinkling
> ½ cup chopped bittersweet chocolate (about 2½ ounces)
> ¾ teaspoon pure vanilla extract
> ¼ teaspoon salt
> 1¼ cups water (room temperature)

1. Combine all the ingredients except the salt and water in the bowl of an electric mixer. (For hand technique, see Technique Note.) Mix with the paddle attachment until the butter is broken up into tiny bits. Switch to the dough hook, add the salt, mix a few more seconds, and add the water gradually with the motor running. Mix on medium-low speed until the dough comes together into a ball. Continue mixing to knead the dough until it is smooth and quite elastic, 8 to 10 minutes. Add a tablespoon or so of flour during kneading if the dough feels sticky.

2. Turn the dough out onto a lightly floured board, divide it in half, and knead each half for a minute or two. Form each half into a smooth ball, stretching the top and tucking the edges under. Place the balls on a sheet pan dusted with flour, dust the tops with a little more flour, and cover them loosely with plastic wrap. Set aside to rise until doubled in bulk, about 45 minutes to 1½ hours depending on temperature.

3. Punch down the dough. Roll each ball into an oval, then roll the oval up into an even cylinder about a foot long, stretching the top until smooth and tucking the ends under to form a neat oval loaf (what the Italians call a *mantovana*). Or, for more interestingly shaped slices, make a braided loaf: flatten the dough by hand into a long oval and cut it lengthwise from near one end into three equal strands attached at the end. Braid the strands and tuck the ends under. Place the loaves on an oiled or parchment-lined baking sheet. Sprinkle the tops with a little sugar, cover, and let rise until doubled again.

4. Preheat the oven to 375°F. Slash the tops of the oval loaves (but not the braided loaves) lengthwise with a razor blade or very sharp knife. Bake the loaves until they form a good crust, but the tops still spring back when lightly pressed, 30 to 35 minutes. Let cool thoroughly before slicing.

Variation: The braided shape is ideal for making a bread pudding, but this dough can also be baked in a loaf pan, in long baguette-style loaves, or in small individual rolls. Slash the tops of rolls or free-standing loaves just before baking.

Technique Note: If you don't have a mixer, cut or rub the butter into the flour in step 1 as if making pie dough and use a wooden spoon to mix in the remaining ingredients. When the dough becomes too stiff to work, turn it out on a floured board and knead by hand. Plan on a good 10 minutes of mixing to get a strong, elastic dough.

HAZELNUT CUSTARD

This hazelnut-flavored custard has a smooth, sensuous texture and a flavor that lingers on the palate without cloying. Although it is perfectly delicious by itself, you can dress it up further with a seasonal fruit garnish. In late winter, for example, you could serve it with slices of blood orange flavored with a little vanilla. In summer, use raspberries or other berries. Or any time of year, try the *crème brulée* treatment given in the variation below.

Makes 8 to 10

> 4 cups cream
> 5 ounces (1¼ cups) ground toasted hazelnuts (see **Note**)
> 5 large egg yolks
> ½ cup sugar
> 2 tablespoons pure vanilla extract
> Pinch of salt

1. Combine the cream and hazelnuts in a saucepan over medium-low heat. Heat gently; adjust the heat to maintain a very low simmer until the cream takes on a strong hazelnut flavor, about 45 minutes.

2. Preheat the oven to 250°F. In a large bowl, beat the egg yolks lightly just until smooth. Add the sugar, vanilla, and salt and mix just until the sugar dissolves; do not beat any more air than necessary into the mixture. Add the hot cream gradually to the egg yolk mixture, stirring constantly. Strain the mixture through a fine nylon sieve or through a wire sieve lined with a double layer of cheesecloth.

3. Pour the custard mixture into 8 or 10 shallow ramekins or custard cups set in a baking pan. Place the pan in the oven and carefully pour in hot water to come halfway up the sides of the ramekins. Bake until the custard is set but still soft, about 2 hours. To test, insert a table knife and spread the custard apart slightly; it should be semisolid, not liquid, but still soft enough that it collapses back into the hole rather than standing up firm. Serve warm or at room temperature.

Note: Toasted and ground hazelnuts are the closest equivalent of the authentic Italian ingredient *farina di noccioli* (literally, hazelnut "flour"). You might find it in well-stocked Italian delicatessens, but it is probably easier to make your own. Toast and skin whole hazelnuts as directed on page 154. Place the skinned nuts in a food processor (or a nut grinder, if you have one) and grind to a fine meal. Do not grind too far or it will become nut butter. Let cool, then store tightly sealed in the refrigerator, where it will keep for several weeks.

Variation: To serve this custard in the style of *crème brulée*, sprinkle the top of each finished custard with about 1 teaspoon of granulated sugar (or superfine sugar, if you have it) and broil it until the sugar melts and caramelizes. When it cools, it will form a thin, crisp shell, which you break into with your spoon to eat.

LEMON
AND WHITE CHOCOLATE
SORBETTO

Like French *sorbet*, *sorbetto* is a frozen dessert made without milk or cream. In this case, the addition of white chocolate gives a richness and smoothness that suggests ice cream.

Makes 2½ pints

- ¾ cup sugar
- 2¼ cups warm water
- 5½ ounces top-quality white chocolate, chopped (see Note)
- ½ cup lemon juice

Combine the sugar and ½ cup of the water in a small saucepan. Heat until the sugar dissolves, a little short of the boiling point. Pour the syrup into a heatproof bowl or the top of a double boiler. Add the chopped chocolate and lemon juice and warm over boiled (not boiling) water, stirring occasionally, until the chocolate melts. Add the remaining 1¾ cups water, strain to remove any unmelted lumps of chocolate, and freeze in an ice cream maker according to the manufacturer's instructions.

Note: White chocolate is not really chocolate, but a confection made of cocoa butter, milk solids, vanilla, and sugar. Be sure you get the real thing, not a cheap version made with other vegetable fats or imitation vanilla. The best brands come from Europe, especially Switzerland. White chocolate goes bad much faster than dark chocolate, so buy it from a source that turns over its stock rapidly, keep it tightly covered, and use it fairly quickly after opening a new package.

INDEX

Italic page numbers indicate photos.
Bold page numbers indicate main entries.

Metric Conversion Table

Follow this chart to convert the measurements in this book to their approximate metric equivalents. The metric amounts have been rounded; the slight variations in the conversion rate will not significantly change the recipes.

Liquid and Dry Volume	Metric Equivalent	Temperature	
		°Fahrenheit	°Celsius
1 teaspoon	5 ml	155	70
1 tablespoon (3 teaspoons)	15 ml	165	75
¼ cup	60 ml	185	85
⅓ cup	80 ml	200	95
½ cup	125 ml	275	135
1 cup	250 ml	300	150
		325	160
Weight		350	175
1 ounce	28 grams	375	190
¼ pound	113 grams	400	205
½ pound	225 grams	450	230
1 pound	450 grams		

Linear

1 inch	2.5 cm

Other Helpful Conversion Factors

Sugar, Rice, Flour	1 teaspoon = 10 grams
	1 cup = 220 grams
Cornstarch, Salt	1 teaspoon = 5 grams
	1 tablespoon = 15 grams

RECIPE

— NOTES —

R E C I P E

— N O T E S —

ABOUT THE AUTHOR

Robert Helstrom has been Executive Chef of Kuleto's Italian Restaurant since 1988, during which time he has traveled extensively in Italy exploring regional Italian cuisines. Prior to coming to Kuleto's he worked for 20 years as cook and chef in a variety of French, American, and Mexican restaurant kitchens. A native of Indiana, he lives in Marin County, California. This is his first book.

ABOUT KULETO'S

Kuleto's Italian Restaurant is one of San Francisco's most popular dining spots. Located at 221 Powell Street just off Union Square, the restaurant serves contemporary Italian food drawn from all regions of Italy, often adding its own intriguing, non-traditional touches. In the pursuit of the finest ingredients, the restaurant makes its own fresh pasta, breads, and desserts daily, cures its own olives and meats on the premises, and has its own brand of olive oil custom bottled in northern California. In a city known for its Italian restaurants, Kuleto's excellent food and warm, inviting atmosphere have made it a favorite with local residents and visitors alike from the day it opened in 1986. For reservations, telephone 415-397-7720.

OTHER COOKBOOKS AVAILABLE
FROM HARLOW & RATNER

THE COOKING OF SINGAPORE: GREAT DISHES
FROM ASIA'S CULINARY CROSSROADS *by Chris Yeo and Joyce Jue*

A cook's guide to the vibrant cuisine of Singapore—a unique blend of Chinese, Malaysian, Indonesian, and Indian traditions, plus the spectacular Nonya cooking style hardly known to American cooks until now. Hardcover, 176 pages including 35 pages of color photos.

EVERYBODY'S WOKKING *by Martin Yan*

Companion book to the ever-popular public television series "Yan Can Cook." A 176-page quality paperback with 35 pages of stunning color photos. Everybody's favorite Chinese cook, Martin Yan makes healthful Chinese cooking simple and fun.

THE WELL-SEASONED WOK *by Martin Yan*

Martin Yan explores more Chinese and Southeast Asian cooking and introduces an assortment of his own East-West dishes. Quality paperback, 192 pages including 31 full-page color photos.

MORE VEGETABLES, PLEASE: DELICIOUS VEGETABLE
SIDE DISHES FOR EVERYDAY MEALS *by Janet Fletcher*

All the home cook needs to know to serve a tasty, nutritious vegetable as part of dinner every day. Includes 34 easy-to-cook vegetables and more than 200 ways to serve them, plus guides to buying, storing, cleaning, and cutting each vegetable. Quality paperback, 228 pages including 32 full-page color photos.

ASIAN APPETIZERS: EASY, EXOTIC
FIRST COURSES TO DRESS UP ANY MEAL *by Joyce Jue*

More than 60 easy-to-prepare dishes that fit nicely into Western menus. The recipes are drawn from China, Thailand, Korea, Japan, Vietnam, Singapore, Indonesia, and the Philippines. Quality paperback, 132 pages including 30 full-page color photos.

Jay Harlow's BEER CUISINE: A COOKBOOK FOR BEER LOVERS

Much of the world's best food goes very, very well with beer. This exuberant collection offers 78 recipes ranging from snacks and nibbles to elegant dinners for company. Includes a summary of beer history and a guide to styles of beer. Quality paperback, 132 pages, including 30 full-page color photos.

HARLOW & RATNER was founded in 1990 to publish high quality cookbooks that are as authoritative and useful as they are beautiful. All of the authors published under the Astolat Books imprint are accomplished professional cooks and cooking teachers. Recipes are true to their ethnic origins and easy to reproduce in the average home kitchen. Astolat Books are for anyone who loves to cook and wants to learn from the best.